MW00715828

A Journey in Words

Discovering My Being

by
Diane E. Peeling

Strategic Book Publishing and Rights Co.

Strategic Book Publishing and Rights Co.
12620 FM 1960, Suite A4-507
Houston, TX 77065

www.sbpra.com

ISBN: 978-1-62857-513-2

Design: Dedicated Book Services, (www.netdbs.com)

Dedication

Here it is, finally! For my sister, Judy, who has hounded me at every opportunity she`s had to know when this was coming out in print, thank you. Over the years, you really never let me forget that I should do this.

BBW, you know I can never thank you enough! I have tried to explain to you the gift you have given me. This is my way of saying and showing my appreciation and understanding. Believing in me and my abilities has not always been simple. You know, "This woman's heart."

Acknowledgements

Over the years I have allowed the disdain on people's faces and my own fear to put my writing on hiatus. My own doubt helped it along and the perfect excuse was, "I was busy living." I am "busy living" today, and the excuse is no longer the crutch. It takes an extraordinary amount of desire sometimes to keep at it.

Inspiration has come at a cost so great that only my universe and the need for balance have forced me to write. It has been my outlet and my saving grace. The universe took away and gave back, and I hope I can truly acknowledge all that has happened.

The influence we have on other people's lives is staggering. We usually are not told or shown. I have been blessed with both.

I write to tell my heart, emotions, and who I was and am becoming, daily.

If I have moved you to think about our humanity, then I did what I intended in my journey inwards.

Diane E. Peeling

Table of Contents

My Note to the Universe

Keep me strong through the difficult times.

Keep me fair through all injustices.

Keep me loving and caring with all the anger and pain.

Keep me calm and sure and guide me on this path of curves.

God, keep me through all uncertainty.

In faith, in love, in pain, in sorrow, always,

GOD KEEP ME!

No Goodbye

December 8, 2010

You left when I was looking right at you.

There were no goodbyes, "I love you," or "It's been nice knowing you."

How do I stop my heart from feeling the bitterness of your disappearance?

You were the yin to my yang.

Sometimes, it may not have seemed that way, but it was.

We held hands through getting into the rhythm of our lives.

We built the home you didn't seem to want when we met.

You seemed happy at the time when we held each other's spirits.

We had issues but seemed to get through the trials.

There was always pleasure in our touches, even when caught by other people.

We laughed at ourselves and with others.

The sharing slowly stopped, and I felt alone and angry because you wouldn't talk.

Little did I know that this disease was literally and figuratively eating you up.

You couldn't tell me something you didn't know, but you didn't ask for help.

When at last the help came, it was too late to stop the roll your body was on.

It was too late to put on the brakes of the emotional roller coaster I was on.

I had been sitting on the highest peak with nowhere to go but straight down.

The devastation that was waiting at the bottom of the drop initially crippled my emotions.

I am neck-deep in that quicksand of emotional starvation, as I know you can't help.

I see you, and you are physically there, but so much less of you.

Underneath the skin and bone that you are now, you seem lost, and I can't reach out and touch your heart anymore.

When I see you, it tears a small piece of me away and re-opens the floodgates of raw emotion.

I have been in a state of inertia since we were told of this robbing disease.

I am so tightly jammed into this arena of helplessness that it has hampered my exercise and opened the pit, eating my ability to allow myself to feel my loss.

Do you know me now, or am I that part of the brain where I have disappeared?

Have I become someone who visits you so you are not to-tally alone, as I feel?

I have all kinds of people around me, yet I feel no less alone than you are.

Friends and family are a blessing at this time, and this would be a lot harder without them,

But they can't replace the intimacy of our marriage, and that is the crux of the matter.

That is what has gone from our marriage, and knowing that only deepens the inertia.

Leather and Strength

October 20, 2011

As my hand passes under my nose, I smell aged leather.

It takes the wear and tear and still looks and feels strong.

Close your eyes, and the suppleness gets under the skin.

Feel the years of wear, oils, and life in the fibres.

The strength of the material becomes a part of the person
wearing it.

Do we stop and touch the leather and sense the strength?

Can we lean into the strength and float on the senses?

Life gets in the way of the small smells, textures, and things
that bring our awareness to the forefront.

In my grief, it has been a smell that slaps me back to the
present and the desire to live daily.

I seem to go weak in the knees when I think of that smell,
and it makes me aware of my own desire to be dressed in
lace.

Sense of Goodbye
October 22, 2011

You have taken a direct step away from our lives.

I missed when you went "Bye," as you did it so quickly,

Your goodbye was so subtle that we missed the moment in time.

Your children are building a foundation with your grand-children.

You missed Morgan's peaceful aura. Did you give your spirit to her as you left?

Watching your children cope with the loss of "Daddy" is beyond sad;

This is why my sense of family is so strong at times.

Now all we have is the thought, the memory, of "Studley" and "Daddy."

You may have had your feelings of being "not there" as they grew, but your heart was never away from them.

I saw the tears of sadness and held you when the reality of life was too much.

Your children will never truly understand some of your heartache about not being there.

You always wanted to be the good guy, even to the detriment of your children.—

Strength and love should be intertwined into one, not a trade-off.

We teach our children the basics and then hope they have the skill to love.

Love was supposed to be the cornerstone of us and the children.

Sometimes it felt like a trade-off—love for attention—if you deemed so at the time.

We pass on the life lessons we learned from our parents to the world, and hopefully, to our children.

If we can hug ourselves and our children, and have them feel and know they are loved, then we have succeeded in our hearts.

Your children may resent you not being there when they thought you should have been (your heart always was).

There was great sadness about you once in a while when you overthought life.

I felt it, and I saw it, but I never truly understood it until now, when you truly are not near.

I see now that when you judged everyone else, you judged yourself more harshly.

You had a hard time expressing your fears and losses; you did head for the great emotional equalizer, and in this instance, it caused great illness.

Your sadness has finally found its out, and the loss is for everyone who loved you, those who still love you, and your children who will never know the man who loved them.

Physical Intuition

October 24, 2011

My body's radar has been in full swing for a while now;

Intuition is only that, if you don't pay any attention.

We all have the sensation of knowing what is going to happen next,

Playing games and choosing without thinking what to throw away,

And the charge of excitement you feel when you move to the draw.

You see it happen but discount the slight nausea in your stomach,

The jump of your pulse when you know you chose wrong,

The negative sense that is put out to the world and your life.

Those personal waves you crash into are the next life, which touches your intuition.

People around you will steal those energies from you as they fight every one of their own instincts.

When we protect our instincts and energies, we keep enough strength to carry us past our lives.

If you doubt your instincts, watch out—

Radar will bounce off a solid mass and return to you.

Are you quick enough to allow your intuition to let you know where the object exists?

Do you follow the imaginary line to its source?

When you arrive at the destination, do you recognize your intuition?

The question is not "why" but "what" crashed into me.

The crash is the opportunity to collect yourself and engage with the universe.

Crashing into the intuition can take many different forms.

The wave may be totally different from how it started.

The intuition is dropped many times along its travels and never examined for the message.

It begins along its new direction of energy until it again crashes into positive or negative energy.

Most intuition gets discounted, as people are intelligent and think they know better than their base energy.

Do we really make the decisions, or is the universe having its way with us?

Intuition is our universe, and if you draw the line from the beginning to now,

A pattern will emerge with your personality, your decisions, your intuitions, and your rights and wrongs, and if you are truly intelligent, your happiness was and is a direct result of your universe having a sense of humour.

David, Goodbye
October 26, 2011

You were that eagle that snatched me when I really wasn't
  looking.

I was told three months before meeting you that you were
  circling.

You were described pretty much exactly how you looked.

The weekend I met you, I knew you were waiting to
  pounce, which you did.

There were no subtleties to your personality—you saw, you
  wanted, you took.

I opened up to you and allowed you to feast on the passion
  that was us.

Was it your innate desire to share in the passion that made
  you a bit of a "Chatty Cathy"?

You told people stuff that a group of women would be hard-
  pressed to talk about.

Secretly, I kind of enjoyed that about you, and it fed my
  own esteem.

You held me while we cuddled three days away and shared
  a few comings and goings.

We laughed, we shared the wine in the yard outside the
  apartment, and we shared the sofa.

For the next ten years, we truly shared each other, despite
  our perceptions of our children.

You wanted to bend me to your guilt about your children,
  but it was a no-go.

Maybe that is when you truly understood my strength.

I would like to think that you enjoyed that strength and were irritated when you couldn't break it (and sometimes you tried).

Anything less wouldn't have been you, and I understood— that was the personality I fell for.

We built, we grew, we loved passionately, and we touched, holding hands daily.

I really don't know when you started your journey away from our life, and yours.

Did I know somewhere deep down that our passionate years were all we were going to have?

Maybe that is why every game of crib in the morning was important;

It kept us in touch with each other. We talked, touched, and loved in that hour before the world intruded on our day.

Physical appearance is nothing when the heart and mind separate with this illness.

You no longer recognize me as the woman who loved you passionately and with all my heart.

It has hurt me deeply, and it is not any easier seeing you leave.

You gave me love, a home we built together, a life, my passion.

Wherever you are, I hope and pray you are safer than you sometimes felt here.

I didn't love you a little; I loved you greatly. Know that in your journey and wherever you are.

My Wolf
October 31, 2011

Has the cry in my heart finally been accepted across the
plains of my life?

My infinity for the aloneness of my nature to capture and
release the spirit.

I have been hearing the cry for most of my life and have
never been able to define the piercing feeling in my soul.

My life has been about finding the outer cry to sate the
feeder in me.

The offering may be raw and bleeding and dropped at his
feet for acceptance.

I have learned that I kept dropping it at the feet of illusion.

The alpha wolf keeps ripping at the tendons to slow and
stop the weak from being fed.

It is my turn to understand and accept the wolf that keeps
scratching my paw.

He has cried for the heart that has been just beyond his real-
ity.

Will he stop hunting and know the offering is at his feet?

Will he drink and eat and know that he has found his mate
across the ages?

The wolf in me has followed my universe and the cry to the
lone wolf.

The wolves in us are gnashing at knowing our spirits are
finally accepted.

It is that spirit that will carry us through the turmoil that is in our heads.

If the wolf strays, will he understand the pull and cry in his heart?

The spirit that bore him is stronger in his heart, now that he is dealing with the cry being answered.

He needs to accept that all she-wolves only want their offspring to be happy.

To a mother, "happy" doesn't mean accepting less than who you are.

The weak wolf has found enough strength to leave the den and the she-wolf to her own devices.

She has cried in pain and sadness that the offering was rejected and spit out.

Her spirit and intuition are still strong enough to survive rather than accept another wolf's poison.

Now she accepts, understands, and is able to eat her own offering and share in the cry she has heard for so long.

She knows she can hunt, fight, offer, take, give, and know she will survive and honour the cry and her spirit.

May the lone wolf be, without ripping its heart out!

They are ones with the cry.

Boots

November 2, 2011

The boots have been hidden in the closet for eighteen years.

Once in a while, if I listened, the need to wear them would creep to the top of my mind.

I would dig them out of the darkness and transform my personality for a few hours.

In those few hours, that old wholeness would return, some peace.

They are so comfortable that, on my feet, the extension is true.

In my soul, I protect my being in those boots.

The sense of stature is forced up and out—

I stand straighter, am longer, and shine.

The boots remind me that I have desires, that I need to move.

The boots kick me in the behind so I don't fall into the trap of someone else's empty promises.

My boots make me consider if I am willing to settle for less than myself once again.

They are scuffed and worn, and the grippers are broken.

They are like me: older, used, and look fabulous in the life of day.

I am a confident, self-assured woman, and my boots force me to recognize that.

Until a couple of days ago, I truly questioned why a pair of boots could change a perception.

My being needs beauty of every kind.

Those boots are an integral part of my protection against things that can and have hurt me.

They are only a pair of boots, yet when I have them on, they transform me into a sexy, beautiful woman in work clothes.

People have noticed me when I wasn't expecting it, as most people don't see.

Wearing those boots moves everything in my soul.

It is about never allowing someone else to tower over me, my heart, my desires, or my life.

Those boots bring out the protector of me,

Revelations can kick you unexpectedly, and now, Mom, I get it.

The Chickadee

November 2, 2011

The chickadee is such a tiny bird yet it survives the harshest weather.

In the past month, they have been next to me.

They have flown directly at me,

Sat next to me on the branch.

One even sat on my elbow when I was standing on my deck.

In my grief and loss and aloneness, this tiny bird kept watch.

It has taken me a while to figure out the watchful chickadee.

As I sit here and write, I realize that it is a thought from Mom.

As I grasp the enormity of the message, the chickadee carries forth.

I know my mother doesn't want me to allow another to steal my being.

I have gone through my life having the opportunity to know my mom as the woman.

Through the chickadee, she has truly given me the answer to her being.

How many generations go by when no one understands what came before?

The chickadee and the universe are smacking us;

Will we get it and allow it to be everything it is?

The chickadee is part of my universe and my daily reality, and I need to thank the significant guidance I have finally recognized.

There are things larger than us out there, and those nuances are what keep us going into our lives.

Nature, our universe, my being, my hopes, wants, needs, desires, and satisfactions have always been in the abstract, which is my uniqueness.

My Grief

November 3, 2011

The grief I let wash over me is almost drowning me in its
  severity.

I was walking when it hit me, and I could have walked for
  hours.

When the stomach-wrenching, throw up feeling grabs a
  hold, it becomes hard to breathe.

It bends you over so that you are standing curled into a ball.

Your breath just sticks in your lungs so that even gulping air
  is difficult.

The hyperventilation and sheer loss of breath make you
  want to run away.

I did the same thing when my mom passed away, as I was
  overwhelmed with the enormity of my loss.

She was the constant in my life, no matter what.

The enormity of the loss of my husband does not lessen the
  years spent, knowing it is the end of us.

This loss makes me angry, as in the end I will grieve alone
  as I did with Mom, as you had already left.

You never really held me in your arms when Mom exited
  this life.

The total of your platitudes to me when I was grieving was,
  "I am sorry"—

No holding me when the grief overwhelmed me,

No loving me long into the night in your arms.

There was plenty of smoking pot for you and more distance for me.

Mom's passing was the catalyst that let me know, deep in my heart, that something was wrong.

You were so loving and kind, warm and giving, when Dad passed away, and I was expecting the same with Mom.

I find myself finally grieving for Mom as well as you, and I do so alone.

There are very few people who truly grieve with you and for you.

Those people are always the ones I least expect to give support freely.

The heartfelt grief they share with you allows you to know you are not alone.

People die, and lives end daily, but there is not one person out there who doesn't feel the aloneness of death.

We say all the words most times, but we pray silently it isn't a direct hit to us.

Human nature is about living, whether or not we like it.

We have numerous chances at living, loving, and making a difference in our own life never mind someone else's.

I will miss you always; we shared so much.

In your leaving and my grief, I will always cherish what we shared, loved, and lost.

You are finding your way, day by day, to a place I do not want to go.

There will be plenty of events on the time continuum before we truly meet again.

I grieve now for myself and my direct loss of everything we were.

I will need my fortitude and strength to support your children when you physically leave.

I am going to move forward into my heart and my life.

There are people here who I need, and they need me (hopefully for a long time to come).

Walk the path to wherever you go and be comforted by the knowledge that you made a difference, and that I am thankful I was in love with you for this long.

I didn't totally forgive you for your treatment of me with my mom, but I now understand the stolen time.

Go with love, peace, joy, music, and an angel always sitting on your shoulder.

Simplistic Patience

November 4, 2011

One line of simple words pushes forth the desired.

The power of those words evokes sheer delight or terror.

The words have their own agenda and insinuate themselves into the willing mind.

A few moments of time to arrange the text so the meaning is clear,

The comfort given by the patience of another,

The emotion taken from the patience of another's few words—

Thinking of that much patience makes the heart race a tiny bit.

Can a heart withstand the continuous urge for another?

Does that patience waiver when there is only the merest response?

In being that simplistically patient, can it hold out through what is being thrown in its path?

Are the odds of that patience being satisfied realistic?

When will human nature kick in and hands be thrown up, and enough will be done?

Is the reality of the object that is being patiently awaited going to be the truth or illusion of long, simplistic patience?

My Child
November 6, 2011

I am blessed with a quiet, together young man.

His sensitivity to those around him is so a part of this person.

He cares so deeply that it cuts to the core of my heart.

He doesn't protect himself from what he gives other people.

He embraces his life with a certain gusto that is rare in this life.

His heart of hearts is his significant other.

Only she knows what the honest cost truly is.

He will go to the ends of the earth for her, to help her feel safe.

He watches, he sees, he does, and he will take care of her heart.

Sometimes, I feel there is terror inside him that he won't do enough.

He needs to let that go and gently become aware of his innate kindness.

He is the caregiver in all his relationships, which makes everyone glad for his presence.

The front is woven so deeply that he doesn't know it's become the armour.

He was part of my being from the first breath I took with him.

The black eye the moment he was born was a strong indicator of his life ahead.

At no time has it been simple and easy for him.

My heart wanted to protect him from the only life we have.

Truly the only protection I could give him was to tell him,
"Be true to yourself."

There are forces out there that will destroy you if you let
them."

I always tried to assure him that regardless of whatever hap-
pens in life, I would be there.

Life parted us temporarily, but a thought was always there
for him.

To this day, I want him to know I treasure my child,

The man that he has become with some pretty stiff guid-
ance at times,

The humour that covers some of the pains of life.

I felt the times when he was hurt and in pain, and I tried the
mother's salve, listening to and reassuring him.

When I feel, know, want, and desire the best for him, I see
it achieved.

We have laughed, cried, and hugged through silence, peace,
joy, sadness, pain, and disappointment, but they all con-
tinued to grow us.

The small part I played along the way makes a woman
happy, a mother proud, a spouse ecstatic, and my life to-
talled.

Pristine Snow

November 12, 2011

I awoke this morning to a home covered in pure, new snow.

It was heavy with moisture and clumped easily.

I grabbed a handful, forced it into a ball, and tossed it away,

One simple gesture to open up my spirit to the clean, white day.

No two snowflakes are the same, but when falling together, they take on a new form.

When warmth is applied to the snow, it melts and cleanses more than just my hands.

Snow symbolizes the next season in my life, when I can rest and renew myself with each new fall of beauty.

Snow allows things to take on new shapes, new meanings, and a fresh, new look.

Look at the newness of everything it has fallen on.

For a few moments before the flakes take on a new shape, stop and enjoy.

It is the breath of our life when we stop for a second in time and see,

Push back from the business of our "to-do" lists, and be.

That first snow reminds me that all things change constantly. Do we know the joy of our life?

Laughter

November 9, 2011

The raw bubble burst from deep in the heart.

It sounded like a minor explosion of pure delight,

Popping out so unexpectedly after many years of being hidden.

The noise was so refreshing that it felt like the mist from a cool spring shower.

My mood is so elevated that I am picking up nuances in the hidden life.

It feels like it should come from the inner child in all of us.

My life has been busy, living, feeding, and worrying about our daily chores,

Why do we cut off our pure laughter?

The ear hears all if we stop and listen past the white noise,

And now I am discovering the laughter that has slipped out over the years.

I am turning down my white noise interference and keeping and hearing the joy of life,

Sharing what I hear with the few people who know the inner life within their own laughter.

This is one step towards total acceptance of the gifts that are given daily.

Grieving the Realities

November 12, 2011

As I walk off some of my frustration, I look inside my-
self—

Am I so shallow in my apparent neediness that I let it eat
me up?

Is this not more of the pattern over the years when you have
faced great loss?

I have been married three times, and the third will be the
widow maker.

Each time my loss has happened, maybe I also lost a tiny bit
of myself.

I have gone through periods of neediness when the loss was
complete in my heart.

I have always come out of those same periods a stronger
person for having wallowed a while in it.

It serves to remind me that the choices may be in our
minds.

They are sometimes not the choices of our intuition and our
universe.

The first was a knee-jerk reaction to my sister hitting on my
ex before we were married.

No one was having him but me, and I am thankful for my
son.

The second was a reaction to his mother complex and the
belief that I could change him;

I understood the addictive personality, so I could help.

The third and last one was my idea of my mate.

With this one, I hit all of the above, including the possible addiction, which his mother warned me about.

He made the right promises, so I allowed myself to ignore my intuition.

I tried to tell myself numerous times, when we went to see my nephew,

When I partially moved to Edmonton and then took the new job in Calgary.

I was determined to know what was right and just overrode my instincts.

I am on my way to learning that your instincts will guide you to where you are actually supposed to be.

I need to enjoy the journey and the stops along the way.

My journey has been anything but quiet and sedate—

My highs have been startling and my lows have been thoughtful in restlessness.

In my lows and highs, you can read the emotions of clarity.

This time, my emotions are laid out flat against my heart;

I need them to bleed out before I go looking for any changes.

In examining where I have been and ignoring my instincts, I need to recognize that my life is where it is supposed to be.

More Grieving

November 12, 2011

The grief seems so intense right now that it is all encompassing.

I need to let go of his heart and let him fly away.

I need to release my heart from the hurt and loss.

Walking releases some of the stressful tension I am wired with.

I could walk for miles if that allowed me to move away from my grief.

I am putting miles on my body and legs, yet the band of tightness is not lessening.

The band may not lessen until I truly let him go away physically.

All hope has been diminished, yet the small flicker still opens the hope.

He has been lost to me for years, yet he hasn't left my being;

A part of him will always be a part of my heart and soul.

I need to set him free as well as myself.

My movement forward is two steps forward and three back.

One day, the forward momentum will be five steps forward and none back.

There will be no fog in my thoughts of David and what we shared.

That would be the pain I am in right now; I can see and feel him so clearly.

I don't have to concentrate on picturing him, as I see both sides of him.

As the wife in me, the picture of health I see is startlingly clear.

As the caretaker in me, I see everything that has been lost.

I know I cannot give him the care he needs or the emotional support.

We were so much a part of each other that I need to protect myself from the loss.

Most days, I succeed at protecting myself, and other days I fail.

No matter whether it is a successful day or not, I know I live.

Today is like a new snow, a fresh start before the loss becomes permanent.

I am not going to rush letting go, as I need to do that in small doses.

I am learning that all I can do is deal with one very small dose of loss at a time.

I will get there when my universe says "Time's up."

I will miss you as I have done for the last five years, and always.

Grieving More

November 14, 2011

Age is of little comfort in the early morning hours.

Fear startles you awake when you are deep in slumber.

The trigger is pulled so gently that you don't see the moment.

A gentle nudge in the brain pokes you to consciousness.

The clock tells you how long you slept before the fear awoke.

I tell myself in prayer each night to watch over those in my sight.

I sense my fear of the unknown time of death.

I know exactly when the first death in our lives happened.

I am fighting acceptance of the final departure.

I have been so wired on fear of death that it has become my crisis.

The edge is becoming thinner with every moment of fear that is allowed.

A deep and desired sleep for more than a couple of hours would lessen the fearful anxiety.

Great friends have listened and talked me down to quietness.

Holding on to some of that quietness seems difficult when I am alone in the early morning hours of wakefulness.

We can tell ourselves we cannot have life without death intellectually,

But in our arrogance, death is always for others.

As I face different auras of death, I wonder, *Have I lived?*

This fear, as it is beginning to show itself, is more about my impact during my life.

Vanity is a nasty little emotion that has emerged from within.

In flying high on the crisis, I am allowing myself the ugliness of that feeling to show.

I am discovering that I have hidden this quality in me under the perceived face.

The fear of acceptance and my success have only been transcended by the many deaths within life.

It is time to accept that I am living completely and that death will arrive in its time.

The time has come when writing is as vital to me as breathing.

Those flashes of fear have finally been productive for me, getting me to accept the death of my own vanity.

My Dogs
November 14, 2011

Sometimes, the greatest gifts come in the cutest packages.

The dog person in me only had a desire for a specific kind.

It had to be a Shih Tzu, as that breed appealed to my appreciation of "different."

The gift came in a rescue package, when they were no longer loved:

One black and white, and one golden-tan and white.

They were perfection, even with one missing an eye.

Those three eyes looked into my soul, and I was forever lost.

They had been discarded to the garage, as they were no longer perfect.

Timing seems to be everything in my life, as we were moving out of the city to the acreage.

These two tiny creatures that stole into my soul could now have space.

I didn't know when I met them and began caring for them the gift I was getting.

The natural fit seemed to be Sassy on my shoulder and Charley on his lap.

They became extensions of my heart, and a look could do me in.

They propagated, having a couple of litters of joyful balls of fur.

31

One day Sassy disappeared from our lives. We were never sure what had happened.

Charley was alone, and I sensed that part of me kick in; he always had a mate.

The last litter they had together, a tiny fur ball had been kept.

A year later, Charley had a friend again, and I didn't feel so alone when I saw the two.

She was golden-tan and white like Charley but had Sassy's soul.

It wasn't long before she found her place on my shoulder.

These three fur balls have loved, cuddled, and protected my being.

As they continue to sense my sadness, they give me a reason to go home.

They greet me, and I know I feel it was a wonderful day.

Some part of me settles down when Shonsey sits on my shoulder and Charley is curled in my lap.

They take me outside myself and allow me to focus on what is important:

My living, their life, my loss, and their gift of purity!

Flirting
November 14, 2011

Innocent flirting has turned from innocence to a pure pleasure—

A single smile, a single twinkle, an uncompromised laugh,

The tiniest pull from another's bottled laughter,

A connection from out of nowhere to give enough attention to notice.

There is no hiding the flirting, as it is in pure fun.

The people doing the flirting know in their subconscious that they are being electrocuted.

Human nature being what it is, we explore the little zaps of electricity.

In our heart of hearts, we know there can be nothing more than zaps.

Life has played out differently than we anticipated when the zap began.

A continuous zap happens daily when we don't speak.

The insanity is not one-sided, as the zap is reflected back.

The touch isn't a small zap but an outright jolt of pleasure,

A caress so light and simple that it lights the nerves on fire.

Long after the caress, the desire burns a trail on the skin.

An innocent flirtation, the not-so-innocent result of total connection.

Hands

November 15/16, 2011

Hands that hold the presence of you in my life,

Hands that are strong but gentle when required,

Fingers that curl and hold the most vulnerable heart,

Palms that marvel that a touch from another palm can be so soothing,

Thumbs that can hook the desire from deep inside.

Hands that grasp another in friendship, in introduction, in a life-altering course,

The hand that guides when one is blinded in the darkness of night,

Fingers that point out some flaws that are better off not judged,

Knuckles that can cause pain when not exercised in patience,

Curled hands that can rap on the edge of the door to your soul.

Hands of beauty know all these things—

Hands of help come in so many sizes and shapes.

The hands can tell so much in a touch if you are aware.

We hold our lives in each other's hands, yet we forget to be gentle and kind.

The hands of my heart tell you to be gentle; they can be scratched and scarred without care.

Take my hand while the journey unfolds and trust the hands of my heart.

A Ray

November 16, 2011

I am standing, watching the pinpricks of light in the sun-
beam.

They are the ice crystals from the cold winter's air,

The tiniest drops of moisture gently falling to earth and dis-
persing.

The sunlight is strong and clear and makes my thoughts be-
come crystallized.

The tracks of my life in the snow and the stories which
could be told . . .

Each small dewdrop of moisture gradually changes the di-
rection of my heart.

The entrances and exits in my life fade with changes.

Some tracks are far deeper than they were when they began.

The past tracks are gradually fading with growth and ac-
ceptance.

Those tracks we remember with pain or delight.

As painful and delightful as they can be, they serve to re-
mind us that we live.

While making those tracks in our lives and others, we were.

The beam has changed ever-so-gently, as I have, while
watching the crystals of change.

We fight the crystals of our lives until we are wise enough
to love ourselves.

In the most drastic crystals and tracks in my life, I am find-
ing my own place.

Awake

November 17, 2011

Once again, it is early morning and life has allowed me to wake.

It has allowed me to make the choice to smile or be overwhelmed by life.

The past few days have led my sanity to write and discover.

I am finally growing into my creative juices.

They are flowing with such force that it is unnerving.

My life has finally settled, so I can concentrate on that part of me.

The settlement has come at a great emotional cost.

Do I belong in the annals with the great writers?

I do understand the cliché of "With the tortured soul comes great creativity"?

Tortured I am not, but fear has stopped a great many people.

Leaving ourselves where comfort has locked us in doubt,

Trusting our intelligence to recognize our passions and act upon them,

Believing that our mind and body work as one when creativity blossoms.

Daisies could be the flower of my writing.

The tiniest bud grows into the complex, intricate, many-faceted beauty that, no matter how many petals are pulled, has a core strong enough to grow and heal.

The solace of aloneness and support of love bring me peace of heart.

Life has thrown me a few challenges, and I have met most with grace.

If there was no grace in the challenges, then I made the choice to keep going.

This intense pleasure of living, accepting, crying, talking, and touching my soul and others is worth my time awake.

Life is about all the senses of being here for the shortest present.

Loving
November 19, 2011

You stepped into my life in the most unusual way.

My heart and mind were busy with living daily.

I didn't know that I left my soul exposed to the elements,

Busy with living and caring for myself, my spouse, our marriage, and our hearts.

It was an innocent remark to lighten the tight band of emotion.

I had become the tightrope of dissecting my needs and desires.

I was painfully aware of the slow emotional starvation that was happening.

What I wasn't aware of was you quietly and firmly poking my being.

You were well aware of the exposed element of my being.

Blinded by something you probably didn't understand yourself, you poked gently.

I was only open to the tiniest dot of information being passed along.

Even processing the information was not happening in the confusion.

I moved in my life, not anyone else's, selfishly and focused,

All while the connection was moving closer to my soul.

Ignorance must be bliss, or maybe that is all it can be now.

At no time during the travelling connection did it register you.

I was too focused on my pain and the devastating loss of my husband.

The connection allowed me a few seconds of sanity occasionally.

Most of this connection occurred every couple of months.

I was clear as to where I was and wanted to be— "Married, until death do us part."

What I wasn't getting was that "death do us part" was already in full swing.

The emotional death had been happening for years, and I was trying to cope.

When the diagnosis finally came, I understood so much the "death of a heart."

This disease stole his heart and everything we shared.

Acceptance has not been easy, and reality has been more difficult.

The ignorance was total. I was in a cocoon of "poor me," privately.

It was the only way to deal with the changes in every part of my life.

I hid on our acreage and quit moving into my life.

The final "death do us part" from him was that he didn't know me, nor did he want the physical soothing touch.

That was the closing of the door on the marriage and what it was.

I knew then that I needed to get moving into my life and being.

It was in that moment that the elements of my soul started the connection.

The connector had been there for years without recognition of being plugged in.

The connection had been understood but where it was was not known.

A little more devastation had to be forthcoming for me to get it.

It took someone not even in my universe to wake me up to living.

Suddenly the connection was made, in the truly most unexpected way.

You finally got the attention of my head, as you were already in my being.

You allowed me to discover what you already knew,

Stepping in front of me for me to see the connection was my reality of beginning to live.

I am going to live and enjoy what I feel and want with my connected mate.

Wisdom may be that sometimes we have the life to love but only ever truly have one connection that surpasses all.

Music

November 20, 2011

Music has always been a note in my ear,

The scale when I needed to slow down and hear,

The soothing inner vibrations to calmness found in peace of quiet.

The hum has been tuned from nature in the instrument.

A piercing tone of purity from water in a glass,

The perfectly pitched tautness of a guitar string,

A bow gently being played across the violin,

The voice of such purity it brings tears to the eyes and joy to a heart—

When I am surrounded by the notes, tunes, and voices, it resonates in my being.

Truly listening to the music means looking into my being.

How do you not want to sway with the flute when quietly listening?

Lyrics can touch so many meanings in your life.

Great love and great sadness may be found in the words.

It is the tones, hum, and the different levels of vibrations that evoke the emotions.

I feel this from my feet up as I am firmly planted in the music of life.

Waiting
November 21, 2011

The many moments disappear while life changes in our midst.

Words don't describe the emptiness of a single word.

Aging happened in those many moments lost to us.

Grasping the moment and shaking it apart to feel,

I feel more alive and potent in my heart than at any other time.

The energy that courses through my being seems rampant.

I do not want to harness and control that feeling.

It truly tunes me into my life that it waits for no one.

There is no running to life, as we are in the very center of it.

My being has never truly waited for anything or anyone.

I have kicked myself along the way when negative energy has caught me unawares.

I am waiting to complete the grieving cycle that was a significant part of my life.

I am waiting to begin a new and exciting story of my life.

The waiting has become blurred, and the lines have become a thick rope.

I am intertwined with those two lines when a little confusion happens.

When I pull them tight, those lines define themselves clearly.

During this wait, I have glimpses and know that I am not waiting.

I am feeling my life as it should be and know the hugest blessing is in writing this.

I have my life, and there is only sharing that intensifies my joyful self.

Storms

December 2, 2011

The wind howled and blew all night with few quiet moments.

Those tiny breaks of peace were when I rested.

With the wind picking up, so did my doubt.

Hearing the trees sway in the breeze enhanced my intensity.

The air flowed through the window with a cold current.

It made throwing the blankets off to cool the angry heat easy.

The questions flowed through my mind with alarming speed,

Harnessing the emotions with the intent to make sense of them.

My tears have become the river of anxiety with roiling whitecaps.

Those whitecaps come with the rapid changes in my life.

I have entered a whorl of rapids that have me caught in an eddy.

Exhaustion takes over, and I let the emotion spin me close to tipping.

The spray from the wind and the whitecaps slaps me hard, back into my life.

Once again, I dig into my being and grasp the heart of me.

I know that if I paddle hard enough, the spinning will stop.

Letting go and leaving it to my heart, I find the calmness.

I will find myself again in the rapids of my life before this
    storm is done.

Trusting me to be heart, health, and love feels dangerous.

Forward momentum is in full swing.

Shore and shelter are but a belief away.

Believe in trust and your heart, as they will keep you
    grounded.

Seven Ts

November 22, 2011

Teasing has led to whole new height of thought.

The simple gestures take on meanings that were not thought of before.

Tempting our imaginations to feel and think,

The possibilities of new feelings, touches, scents, fun,

Tantalizing the edges of our senses to stretch further,

The awareness that every sense is so close to satisfaction,

Tormenting the feelings to full-blown desire,

Watching the reflection to see the desired reaction,

Taunting the touch, smell, sight, and hearing and imagining the taste.

The idea that our thoughts can be activated so simply,

Tasting all the possibilities of what began as a connection,

Savouring every moment derived from the slow boil of heat,

Torturing each other when apart, testing the bounds of need,

Knowing one touch, a look, a moment could make our hearts bleed—

Everyone needs the seven "Ts" of mutuality for one another in their life.

Senses

November 24, 2011

Listening with your inner ear, you can hear possibilities of
the heart.

Watching with your mind through your eyes, you see into
another's soul.

Feeling the air move quietly around your space,

It whispers and caresses your longing to be close,

Pushing away from ourselves to empty our pent up ener-
gies,

Pulling another's energy and intuition into your realm.

The simplest odour triggers intense emotions,

Every instinct in the fight or flight sensibilities.

We are miles away before we stop and see the emptiness.

Returning to where we started takes enormous effort.

Starting over seems a hurdle I cannot leap over one more
time.

Starting anew allows us to change and become fully ca-
pable beings.

As we tasted and bit into our lives along the way, some
things were hard to swallow.

Bitterness may have become the taste of choice;

Sweetness came to the surface only when necessary.

Sourness we found in the most devastating times.

Textures all of a sudden slipped and slid and grated our pal-
ate of choice.

The perfect bite of our life is when we wake and begin
anew.

Freshness is every morning when we mix our hearts in love.

Emotions

November 25, 2011

Our range of emotions can have a devastating effect on our psyche.

There is no high like being in love with someone.

The reaction to that high is the extreme low in the loss of love.

In the beginning, there was closeness that couldn't be parted.

The desire to be in that someone's aura is negated by being in their presence.

Looks are melded into one when the heart opens.

As we grow and change are we aware of love and the maturity of that sensation.

Hearts are what sustain that flooded feeling of warmth,

But actions can deteriorate the immense joy of loving.

Words can cut and heal some of the actions, but not before the bleeding begins.

Healing the bleeding takes more ability than words or actions.

When the heart and head unite to continue to bleed until the death of love,

There is no changing what has happened, only the ability to move forward.

Were the emotions what carried you to crippling effects of change?

Aloneness can heal the sore and tired heart of someone else's wound.

Opening our hearts, beings, and our wholeness is what will move us to loving again.

It will be different but it will have the devastating effects on our psyche, as all honesty in feelings has on our beings.

Obligations

November 27, 2011

In our daily living there are obligations of many kinds.

Obligations can be a choking emotion when that is all there is to feel.

Being born is the ultimate obligation to love life.

Baby: our obligation to smile and be cute and wonderful to our parents.

Child: we are obligated to learn all there is to know about reading, writing, and rudimentary art of communication.

Child: we are obligated to continue to be charming to all.

Child: sometimes we can break out of the obligation and show joy to all in being.

Teen: we are obligated to grow past our hormones which we know nothing about.

Teen: we are obligated to know what there is to know about sex.

Teen: we are obligated to push past our insecurities and most times without strong guidance.

Teen: we are obligated to make choices about what to do with rest of our lives.

Teen: we are obligated to not totally destroy our parents' sanity.

Young adult: we are obligated to make sure no one gets pregnant in the hormone insanity.

Young adult: we are obligated to higher education when we do not know what we want.

Young adult: we are obligated to go out and find a job and live.

Young adult: we are obligated to choose the direction of our lives.

Young adult: the obligation can choke the choices and livelihood from the educated mind.

Lover: we are obligated to be together and choose how.

Lover: we are obligated to think first of the lover of choice.

Lover: we are obligated to think of the other person first so as not to hurt.

Lover: we are obligated to choose the next level with them or move on to the next one.

Lover: we are obligated to understand what and where we want to go.

Parent: we are obligated to make money to be able to survive.

Parent: we are obligated to ensure there is food on table and substance in the home.

Parent: we are obligated to teach and nurture what we brought into this world.

Parent, lover, baby, child, young adult: we are obligated to be a family with love in our hearts,

Obligated daily to everyone and everything else, and the toll begins to show.

In new love and passion the obligation begins to show rapidly.

Pulling back on the obligation is very difficult, as it has already hooked the freedom of hearts.

In the obligation of living we have totally dismissed the one obligation, the most important one:

The obligation to ourselves is to be happy within, as this is the only emotion that erases the negativity of obligation.

Honour

December 1, 2011

In the cold light of day we honour our employment.

We are there daily, as it provides us with a livelihood.

In honour, we do what we think best for our family.

We share our bounty, ourselves, our time.

In honour, we think of what we need to enrich our lives.

We strive to achieve the goal of enough.

In honour, of our parents we consider the effects of our actions on all they have taught us.

We go out of our way not to disappoint them but not ourselves.

In honour, we live our lives at the judgment of others.

We stop looking in the mirror and asking what we want.

In honour, we quit asking ourselves how we feel.

We are busy doing the living and the necessities.

In honour, we put our children on pedestals that are cracked and unstable.

We stop thinking logically about what is truly best for them.

In honour, we have a pretense of knowing what is best for our children.

We forget mistakes are what make our children and ourselves grow.

In honour of what we have accumulated in our lives,

We give only what the expectations of others want.

In honour, we use the term when difficult choices need to be made.

We ostracise our well-being and health to accommodate a word.

In honour we try to live up to the meaning of that word in our lives.

What we don't do and should is honour ourselves.

We need to honour our beings, our happiness, and our hearts, as this shows true honour to others.

My Prose

December 4, 2011

Words flowed intensely onto the paper without hesitation.

Thoughts of confusion are only clear when words are pouring forth.

Clarity becomes part of the writing in a simple, single word.

Doubts are sorted through and questioned of importance.

Fears seem to override all intelligent information processing.

Emotions shoot short blasts of feelings at the heart.

Writing releases the terrors of the unknown.

All becomes an order of comprehension in my being.

Priorities find themselves in the order of maturity.

Putting the words on paper makes the senses of life a reality.

Anger can be all consuming until it is part of the paper.

Once written, it can be read as much as necessary.

Reading the words, the thoughts, the ideas, releases them to the universe.

Writing has been like drinking water for others.

It has been ignored and neglected throughout my life.

Writing has also been my saving grace when all intelligence left temporarily.

The journals and prose kept my soul and heart safe.

Prose has helped me tell my parent how I felt.

My father gave me the gift of a lifetime when I felt the effect of a simple piece of prose.

My prose has touched and enhanced me, friends, and family.

My personal question has been "Is this good enough?"

Once on paper I know the answer is in every piece of prose I write.

Solidity

December 4, 2011

When I get close to your aura, I feel its consuming intensity.

The aura draws me closer to the light you have shone directly in my heart.

Hesitation pulls me back away from that light.

A solid wall stops me from backing away from my own intensity.

That wall and counter, desk, whatever solid object, allows me some distance.

The distance is usually no more than three steps.

This is enough to allow me to bask in your aura.

When pressed firmly against my physical wall I feel in control of my heart.

I have found myself holding the door against my spine.

My hands need to stay busy when you begin to open the light.

When the light begins to burn slowly it grabs my aura,

And I am drawn into your aura in one very quick moment.

My strength to pull away from the feeling is totally lost in three steps.

As our auras blend into one very bright, blinding light,

I am forever lost in the feeling of your arms holding me tightly.

How is so much gentleness felt in my arms?

In my presence I go into the full tug of war to touch, smell, feel, you and us.

The first kiss of touching melts the rope in the tug.

Your intense blue eyes laugh and see the hesitation of my body.

They also see the love and desire I have and hide only when I have to.

We are aware of our surroundings yet know there is great love in our auras.

Those three steps will be there until the future unfolds and you erase them.

I have to acknowledge that those three steps are mine as well.

The future is in the hands and hearts of time.

We are so entwined in one another's auras that we feel complete.

Acknowledging the love and honesty ties my heart closer to yours.

The beacon you lit a while ago has never let up and I didn't comprehend the pull.

The solidity pressed against my back has kept me just at the edge of your aura.

When we finally travel totally in one another's aura the solidity will disappear.

We have such small pieces of the love we both have for completion—

My hazel eyes, your blue eyes, and the eyes of our hearts know us in the distinction of two becoming one in love.

For Delores

2008

May this small token help this wondrous journey you are embarking on.

I know your faith will sustain you during many scary moments for you and your family along the way.

Sometimes you may feel alone, but know you are not.

My thoughts and prayers are with you always.

Know there are many angels here with you daily.

You are blessed with five special bright lights in your life.

You have been the beacon that was a safe place in their hearts.

Angels are calling you past this haven to join them so you can watch over them all at once.

God keep you close. You will always be in our hearts.

Safe passage!

Her

December 6, 2011

In tears the pain of joy and loss can be blurred.

Watching the tears roll down her cheeks, the emotional
woman emerges.

She is aware of the sensation of knowing how to heal,

The pain of intense feelings for herself, her child, her
friends, her love.

Once she releases the heart of her to the world,

She does not hesitate to allow her being to touch,

Believing in her instinct and intuition she follows where
they lead.

The path has only ever turned around on itself once.

Unerring in her direction of herself,

She follows the invisible path that is intrinsic of who she is.

Romance is such an integral part of her psyche.

She finds the beauty in all things that she embraces.

There is no little bit of anything with this woman.

She will overwhelm your senses and a part of you, ques-
tions the whisper,

The invisible state of being when she touches your human-
ity,

The desire so strong, close is not close enough,

She will bring you to the edge of your being.

There is sensation in knowing you have been forever
changed by knowing her.

Smoochie

December 6, 2011

Smoochie is tall, broad-shouldered, narrow-hipped, barrel-chested, long-legged, tight-butted, blue-eyed, salt and peppered, tasty morsel of a man.

Smoochie has hands and fingers that could make a grown woman cry with desire and lust.

Smoochie can and does have the secret to coaxing the passion to new heights.

Smoochie likes to stick the warm, wet, pink tongue of his just far enough out that it tickles the tip of a passionate woman.

Smoochie likes to play with his desire and test the bounds of ecstasy that he is able to evoke.

Smoochie has a clear idea of what fire he is playing with but just can't help himself.

Smoochie looks into the hazel-eyed, sensitive, lustful, bashful, secret inner heart of his prey and touches.

When Smoochie puts oxygen near his flame there will be an explosion if left too long.

Smoochie has an affinity to engineer what he touches and holds to improve the resulting design.

Smoochie continues to study the object while his mind follows his tongue to soft warm peaks.

Smoochie doesn't rest while the object he desires comes to fruition.

Smoochie enjoys the fruits of his labours when he breathes in the scent of lust.

Smoochie is enjoying the desired effects of the pursuit and has found a heart that nurtures.

Smoochie knows the heart is a fragile thing, as his has been bruised along the way.

Smoochie needs to know that his pursuit will not bruise it again.

Smoochie, your strength and desire is a thought away anytime you need the trust.

Smoochie contains his pain with distractions until it slips and cracks.

Smoochie has to know all in our universe is the way it should be.

Smoochie, all will become clear when you let go and set your heart free to its love.

Smoochie, please trust your heart to lead you to where you are supposed to be.

Smoochie can control only what is in his grasp but he doesn't realize he is choking his being.

Smoochie forgets that life's lessons are not always what they appear to be.

Smoochie can feel the tug of direction coming from afar but doesn't totally trust the warmth from it.

Smoochie, feel what you feel. Denying it will only serve to be a catalyst of unhappiness.

Smoochie, when you chose the pursuit, did you understand where the push came from?

Smoochie has been guided by something far greater than us to be here.

Smoochie patiently waited and was guided by outside strength when to push and when to wait.

Smoochie's eyes marvel when in proximity to what is truly in his heart.

Smoochie really does need to feel, not to ignore the happiness that surrounds his heart.

Smoochie has obligations, as all people do, and he will fulfill those.

Smoochie, someone loves you more than you will ever know.

Smoochie, you are in my heart and have been forever. We just never arrived till now.

Smoochie, we have played at love and have some stunning results in our children.

Smoochie, as with all things, we love our children, but that is why we teach, love, and then let them go.

Smoochie, don't hide your adult love. She wants and will treasure it always.

Wishes

December 10, 2011

Ideas begin in the recesses of the mind,

Once run across our thoughts they begin their journey.

Coincidences happen after the thought was acknowledged.

The tiniest changes begin with the energy of breathing.

Circumstance suddenly change the pattern which had begun.

To the unaware, no attention is paid to what changed.

Reality steps up and we find the change happened.

In our secret mind, was the wish made without acknowledgement?

Was a simple idea waiting on the edge of our consciousness?

Thinking about the possibilities was terrifying.

In that thought, were you putting it out there for the person you were staring at?

The thought was caught and acknowledged by the other energy.

Originally the idea was the simplest process of tossing out the energy.

Receiving the message was easy, but ignored.

Achieving the insight when the universe is spilling forth information

Cleaning up those energies of ideas needs be done immediately.

Some part of those wishes suddenly appear to happen.

This is our cue that the circumstance we find is about us choosing.

Answer the wish from the heart, as that is how it becomes true reality.

The final choice in the wish is whether we believe in ourselves enough to change or accept the circumstance.

Nora

April 3, 1993

The twists and turns of life's cycle were needed at times of
    turmoil.

You have been the helping hand.

We struggled and kept one another living.

There were times it felt it wasn't fun.

We laughed and cried and just held on.

The moments of mistiness were in closeness.

You were the heartbeat of friendship.

We saw one another's pain and happiness.

We shared our life's greatest love.

We became friends and partners in our souls.

We knew each other's faults and positives.

The ties we built can never be severed.

We felt no envy or greed.

This is the best in our growth.

In my heart, you are a part of me.

The love for you, my friend, has been the most pleasant.

Go forth to love and sheer joy.

Your friend and comrade will always be next to your heart.

Living
1993

The crises in our lives deepen our sensibilities.

We nurture our anger and let it feed on our beings.

We keep trying to obtain our ultimate best.

We let the smallest pleasure and touch go unnoticed.

Acknowledgement of another human being is missed.

The lines on our face tell our stories.

The plot, excitement, sadness, and adventure are etched on an oilskin.

We find our stories are no different than those of others.

Only some stories are filled with laughter, honesty, and joy.

The painful stories are buried or carried forward to know only sadness and fright.

The fearful go toward never taking a rest.

As the lines deepen, so do our memories.

Limiting the giving of life slows the story of living.

Falling

December 15, 2011

Joy came into our hearts when we needed it the most.

I have laughed till I cried at the wit that has been exchanged.

Fear has turned to absolute terror when thoughts of aloneness develop.

Pinnacles are so high the drop seems like a free fall of nausea.

Jagged edges poke you hard on the way to the bottom.

A snag on one of those edges can make you catch your breath.

You breathe a thought in the hesitation, the landing will be gentle.

As the fall begins again the nausea tells you it is going to be rough.

How hard you crash will be a direct result of swallowing the terror.

Landing on our feet from the fall lets us release our certainty.

We know the free fall will end as we know the moment has ended,

When the dust is brushed off and we stand straight.

We acknowledge the pure, joyful insanity of love.

The moments of this insanity can only be triggered by the pheromones of nature.

Question your heart all you want. Nature will still guide
your being.

Strength in yourself is how you are loved in our moments of
life.

Strength always finds strength and if it doesn't, the ties that
bind will break eventually.

In the break a weight is lifted so the insanity of living mo-
ments can be acknowledged.

Changing is the strength in yourself.

Accepting this nuance is the freedom to be.

Pillars

December 17, 2011

The striations in the pillar could be many things.

In time, has the pillar oxidized and become weakened?

Has the limestone and granite kept its integrity over time?

Has the striation become deterioration with time?

Has the discolouring only added beauty with age?

Has the groove that is worn weathered aggressively?

Have the hairline cracks collected moisture and deepened the instability?

Has time lessened the pillar's ability to stand true?

Has the pillar become powder in the center with neglect?

Has the pillar held too many fortresses from crumbling?

Has another fortress been added on to the pillar?

Has the load-bearing pillar begun to sway from weight?

Has the pillar changed its stability with each new striation?

Has the pillar become beautiful marble hardened by pressure?

Has the gloss of continuous buffing on the pillar callously petrified its ability to stand true?

The pillar symbolizes an unmovable object that can be leaned on at all times.

Too much leaning and the pillar standing alone will topple unexpectedly.

The lean of the pillar is a few degrees further than it should be.

Does the pillar have the ability to recognize another has been placed next to it?

There is no gloss on this pillar, just the granite of survival.

Where once there was one pillar, there is now the support of another.

The striations are the beauty of time, which enhances both of the pillars' ability to stand in all life's weathers.

Purposes
December 20, 2011

All purposes for touching another's life become clear only
with time.

A question asked at the time when we are ready to hear the
answer,

A word spoken out of turn that the purpose listens to . . .

Help can be at your fingertips when a line is thrown out.

A lifetime of hiding and not wanting to change doesn't im-
prove you.

Can we allow outside influence to trust and not judge?

When the hand up is given, do you take it and hold until the
purpose has been resolved?

Was the hand quick enough to abate any permanent issues?

A blind eye may serve the purpose to clear our thoughts.

As the thoughts clarify themselves the eye should open and
see.

When suddenly seeing it takes the courage of honesty to
make it right.

The courage is as simple as saying a few words on purpose.

In the about face, courage can be drawn from the experi-
ence.

Upon opening the eye, hearing the words, and feeling the
pain, you take the steps of correction.

Release the anguish to cleanse the knot of pure purpose.

Purposes are finally becoming clear as you step into your heart.

Safety for another has finally been released so you can now breathe.

The left turn was firm and hard in its purpose, as courage and energy were needed by another.

The purpose is only partially complete and courage needs to be found within.

The gift has only been the start. The present is in the heart.

Christmas

December 26, 2011

The season of celebration is a few short weeks.

Christmas means many different things to every one of us.

To me, this season means something very different every year.

For me, for many years it meant travelling, as was the expectation.

Respect for our parents and the pleasure to have family around.

Every few years I had my own family in my home to enjoy the time.

Shortbread was the staple baked food and there was always plenty to go around.

My gift truly was the cooking and baking up till the celebration.

The time used for doing this was my reflection time of how truly full my life was.

My family may not have understood who I was as a mother, a sister, a woman, a friend.

At Christmas, when I baked and saw the joy in a simple cookie,

For the moment I had my gift of my heart, as it was in the time.

Gifts have always been minimal and giving something they wanted was far easier than seeing disappointment.

Giving up something precious to you so that those precious to you may have a gift is a lesson of importance.

That gift is my annual reminder what this holiday truly means.

In my travels one year a complete stranger to me, opened her home and Christmas welcomed the lone woman.

The gift of a pair of pantyhose during her family's gift opening was her spirit welcoming all in, and there was enough for everyone.

She had no warning that I would be arriving, as the surprise was total when I got off the bus Christmas morn.

My sister did not know I was coming either, as I left my life there.

This stranger was my sister's friend, so totally alone I was not.

Aloneness can be subjective, as I had to deliver my son to his father to ensure both of our safety.

The beating may have been mine to take and the lesson of our safety was immediate.

We all do things that we look upon now and know that our spirits are far smarter than we are most times.

They will lead us to safety, peace of heart, and every once in a while a true life lesson.

Since that Christmas the smallest, most insignificant gift to you can take on a life of its own in someone else's heart.

It is not the number of gifts, price of the gifts, receiver of the gifts, or the givers of the gifts.

It is the thought of another life and a moment in the present that is passed on in time.

Many years have passed since that Christmas present, yet it remains the milestone of what the holidays are meant to be.

Family has gathered at this time to be together and exchange gifts and time.

Friends wish all the best and have the unique gift of being in the present all year.

When my travels at Christmas take me anywhere, those pantyhose remind me that you never know where the gift will come from if your heart is open to receiving.

Alicia Vows to My Husband

A wonderful, precious gift was handed to me the day we met.

The angels smiled upon our hearts one beautiful summer day, and tied my love to you.

The treasures of my life were few until the angels brought a precious love for you.

With patience, understanding, honor, and desire, I will grow with our love.

I promise to love you throughout my life.

The dream I walk in is forever shared with love and devotion.

The aura changed dramatically since you walked into my life and I smiled in my heart, and it has a permanent place in my life.

Amazement still leaps into my heart when I look at you.

—Alicia Duhault

Deception

December 29, 2011

A word fraught with so many tales of woe.

The tale began with a decision of perceived distance.

Perception changed when the tale became truth.

From afar there was no sight for a change.

The distance became the catalyst to indifference.

Indifference with time became acceptance,

Acceptance came with ignorance while living.

Ignorance is the excuse to hide from acknowledgment of something being wrong.

Acknowledgment for another's pain is drowned in self-preservation.

Self-preservation for every person is totally different in handling the woe.

"Woe is me," yet if you feel that you know you are missing the basics of another's connection.

Deliberately causing another's anguish and pain was not the intention.

The intention was to feel again for the loss of the vow of one.

Vows are taken with the understanding that they are said with honesty.

Honesty within is always the benchmark of happiness,

Happiness changes with every life change if we recognize our maturity.

Deceit was not the idea when it began.

Deceiving yourself is an act no less miserable than being deceitful, as we know the truth shows itself.

Deception is the secret death of what was, and understanding that is when drastic change happens.

Secrets of woe change when faced with honesty and integrity and the paths are cleared of obstacles.

Leaping into your life and out of deception allows all whom you touch freedom from wondering, including yourself.

Enchanting

December 30, 2011

Some old world ideas are brought forth to a new age.

It seems that this concept was left behind in the rush to change.

We have changed our views on the importance of anything enchanting in our daily living.

Our lives are so fast paced that when we slow down, we sleep.

In slowing down, do we feel the earth and all its enchanting gifts?

There is headiness to seeing a floral garden in all its colour,

When the hummingbird flits from blossom to succulent blossom,

Trying to un-focus your eyes so you can see the wings move,

In smelling the dirt, the mold, the grass, and the sharpness of each blade,

Placing a blade of grass between your thumbs to make a whistle,

And the enchanting moment when the whistle sounds.

In the quiet of dusk the millions of insects feed and are fed.

The racket of crickets before your ear tunes to the right tone.

The swoosh of the bats just before the final moment from dusk to night.

Sitting in the enchantment of the day to breathe, to appreci-
ate,

The smile on the face of a baby which we call cute, but
truly the life is the true enchantment.

When our hearts are full of our enchanting lives, we label
the moment incorrectly.

Enchanting life is, as living should be, a pleasure to behold.

Whether a friend, an insect, a flower, or the dirt, we find
many enchanting ideas and moments in our lives.

Look only immediately in front of you and in your heart.

2011

December 31, 2011

It began with special people and a very best friend.

There was one missing but that one could only be held in our hearts.

A toast to the coming year and well wishes for all held dear.

A simple book was brought into my home and left open for me to read.

The story told a million times, but this time it focused on me.

I thought, I read, and I thought again of all it was allowing me to see.

The idea was recognized that it was time for me to flee.

The chain of harm to my health and my being finally broke free,

A rest was welcome but only in my life, as the disease had a hold of half of the whole.

When I saw half of the whole it became a stronger share of the half.

Watching the rapid gain of the loss, the whole diminished.

The picture has stayed the same with the whole half.

The reconciliation of the half that has disappeared still fought the acceptance.

Somewhere in being smaller it allowed the focus to stay clear in the picture.

The grief burst forth with a power of pressure.

There was no more holding back the change in the whole.

Change happened rapidly with the necessity to overcome the tide of emotion.

In the deluge of grief came the strangest life line in the most unexpected form.

With the dawning of understanding came escape from the intensity of the changes being faced.

A deep breath was taken and the landscape shifted to living again.

The swing of opposite sides of the spectrum had taken a while to understand.

There were a couple more surprises and the load felt heavy with changes.

The surprises of those lives that left us too soon made me look beyond my view and see the value of living every day.

The tragedies, the losses, the loves, the pains, the growth, and the creativity make me realize how gifted my life is.

Throughout this year I was overwhelmed with so much emotion I didn't know how to release the energy.

Opening my mind to the possibilities and the energy, the universe, and me, I was shown how wonderful the year has been:

Bittersweet memories, loving thoughts, and a clearer understanding of how connected life can be!

Perseverance

January 2, 2012

The grey cloud rolls across the sky, heavy with rain.

As the thunder claps and lightning flashes menacingly towards the earth,

A piece of black dirt opened itself to receive the shower it needed.

Hours later, there was still no shower for the dirt to nourish itself.

As it pulled the dry blanket back across itself, it rested.

The sun peeked out and blazed a beam of pure light on the blanket of dirt.

The wind picked up and tried to carry the blanket from the dirt to rob its nourishment.

The dirt held on to its protective covering, as it knew what was coming.

A grey cloud peaked with the heaviness of its moisture and whispered to throw back the cover.

Trusting the moisture to shower the dirt with purity, it opened up with certainty.

Dampening the cover was all that was needed to fertilize the dirt.

It welcomed the seed and wrapped it tightly in its blanket to hatch.

The seed of perseverance held its own till it felt the germinator kick off its bran.

The sun shining regularly on the small seed pushed its
growth slowly.

Starches broke down to feed the growth of a new plant.

The blanket of dirt continued to hold it close and give it the
strength to grow straight up.

An occasional drink of moisture, lots of warm sunshine,
and a bit of playful wind for life to persevere.

Harvesting the seeds of perseverance and feeding the seeds
of life, we eat at the table of nature.

Temptation

January 2, 2012

Tasting the sweetness of something delicious and taboo,

Life has so many things that are sweet when consumed in moderation.

Is the temptation to overindulge a naturally bad choice?

Choosing to look past the indulgence to what lies beneath—

The temptation to be out in the sun at risk of getting burned—

We risk the chance because the heat permeates our bodies and we want more.

The temptation to sink our teeth in a warm apple pie after the first piece,

We eat the second piece because we want the taste and smell to last a little longer.

Temptation to caress the petal of a flower and pull on it at the same time,

We see the beauty of the flower but we want to feel the beauty of the petal.

Temptation of more must be better in our daily living.

More spice of life does not improve the quality of you.

Temptations are all around us and that is one desire that will bite you if you let it.

A quick fix when being tempted will surely cause you grief.

As with most temptations in life, it is within you to choose.

Sometimes what seems like temptation is not that at all, but life kicking you to choose.

Every day there is a temptation of some kind to avoid, choose, or ignore.

In doing all of these, the temptation is still there to be faced.

The daily temptations begin in the early morning with wakefulness.

It is late night when sleep is upon us when we have the silence of temptation.

Compassion

January 5, 2012

Where in our heart and our head is our ability to touch another's life?

Do the moments we spend expressing ourselves to another make a difference?

Can we step away from ourselves and who we are to touch another's soul?

Sharing the tears of sadness shows empathy for the loss.

There is no weakness of spirit when pain is shared.

Radical changes happen in our lives without notice and we seek our fellow man for assurance.

The touch of a friend's hand held in steadfast support allows us to feel.

The pain and anguish that are tearing at our hearts heals a bit.

When we look and see humanity, we understand we are not alone in the changes.

Do we take what is given freely and give to someone else during their time of need?

Words only convey our heads, but the hug and the touch release our hearts to what is cherished.

When we accept what we give, then we can pass true compassion into the circle of our life.

No life is truly lived to its fullest without knowing it.

Solitude

January 5, 2012

The quiet surrounds you in a blanket of peace.

The thoughts of aloneness seem less intense.

Being one on one with yourself, you begin to hear your life.

The temperature of your body can change a few degrees when resting.

Taking a deep breath can release the building of stress.

Keep yourself focused on why you want the solitude.

When alone, we can ask ourselves those difficult questions.

There is no judgment from an outside source to interrupt who you are at the moment.

Organization from within begins its journey to answering the ideas.

Removing the noise from the world around you, rest starts.

In solitude you can see the changes in light and feel the shift within.

A sound will become clearer in the silence of the moment.

A problem may crystalize itself in the answer when the mind has eased itself open.

We reduce the white noise of our lives in the precious times of aloneness.

Tinkering during solitude gives our brain waves a chance to bounce around our ideas.

Accomplishments sometimes are the direct result of the action of inaction.

We soar in solitude, as this is a gift we have to give ourselves to replenish what other people take indiscriminately.

When your body and being ache from the grind in your daily life, dealing with people and things,

Collect your solitude around you like a warm and trusted friend and bask in its healing powers.

A minute or hour, just enjoy the time with you.

Hands II

January 5, 2012

The perfect pair of hands hold the stories of many.

They hold and grasp the fingers of Mom and Dad.

They tug and pull on our hair until others pull back.

They grab their toes and other parts in discovery.

They caress the skin with the soothing ability to calm.

They stroke till sleep takes over the mind.

They hold tight the night through in security.

They grip together so all who feel notice the strength.

They can cause a great deal of pain if not watchful.

They give daily the nourishment of health.

They say hello as well as goodbye during our daily routine.

They praise and do well when necessary.

They are the extensions of our senses when we close our
eyes.

They are gentleness when someone hurts.

They are so many things at once that we lose count.

The tips of fingers to the wide palms of hands carry our
lives.

They touch so many in any one day that we sometimes for-
get their value.

They are sometimes smooth, rough, and gnarled all at the
same time.

This just tells a deeper story of where they have been.

The shape of the hand is a truth stronger than words.

Working hands, no matter what they toil at, bring life and laughter to all.

There is nothing simple about our hands, but the attitude behind them.

The hands that give love will take love and freely hand it over, hand over hand.

Exploitation

January 6, 2012

The most innocuous moment in one's life can become a
point of cruelty.

They are moments you would like to hide from, especially
if seen,

Hoping no one notices even when they are directly in front
of you.

Embarrassing as it is to pick yourself up with some dignity
and still smile,

As the memory of that particular moment passes into obliv-
ion it becomes part of you and you smile.

Someone can pick that particular moment and poke the
memory.

Once, maybe twice, it can be funny to laugh with someone
about.

The times after that can become a point of exploitation of a
person.

We need to stop what sounds like ribbing to us and see the
effect on another.

Is the cruelty of exploitation a learned trait when battered
continuously?

When we do that to another person are we striking back at
the exploitation done to us?

We need to stop and hear what is behind the nuances in the
laughter.

Understanding what you are saying and doing to another
person may be so different than you perceive.

Continuously exploiting a person without knowledge or
care is mean-spirited.

The challenge is watching and knowing who and what is
being exploited.

The gain from doing this is checking the damage before it's
done.

Rainbows

January 7, 2012

As the primary colours reach a band across the sky, we are in awe.

As the mist from the rain quiets to a heavy moisture, the colours begin to change.

The barometer begins to move so slowly, and if the atmosphere pours forth more precipitation a second may appear.

Wonderment is in our eyes and in our bodies when we see such beauty.

It makes you feel you can reach out and touch the colours.

When you look closely at the rainbow you can see the nature behind the spectrum.

The arc across the sky makes you hope all dreams and wishes can come true.

Our love in time lets us believe (or want to) that the pot of gold is at the end.

At the age of acceptance we know what the pot of gold actually is—

It is a life of hard work, smart decisions, and following our dreams and desires.

Any time in the life of the rainbow things gradually take on new shapes and meanings.

The colours are definite and then the pressure from within fades the colours and something new appears.

Directions take on new ideas as the previous ones fade away, like the rainbow as the barometric pressure changes the sky.

We understand that the rainbows of our lives are our changes, our acceptance, and the pot of gold while we grew and changed with living.

Memories

January 7, 2012

We smile and laugh at the pictures that flow within our
  minds.

We hear the wonder as the frames go from beginning to
  end.

We see the family that has so influenced who we are,

The time spent with brothers and sisters tormenting each
  other,

Feeling the gifts from strong parents during their guidance
  of growth,

The bruises that suddenly appeared when we tripped and
  fell and got up and brushed ourselves off.

Gathering around the table for dinner and time spent with
  family, warm memories emerge.

The triggers that set off a deluge of memories are most
  times steeped in our early years until we leave home.

Notions that one is more spoiled than the others,

Learning with the teenage years of what can we put over
  Mom and Dad.

As we learn with our children, we had nothing on Mom and
  Dad, as history repeats itself. Their own growth was a
  different version,

Hair raising times, when thought of now, you wonder how
  we survived.

Climbing on the highest peak of the hay wagon just to feel the rush of adrenaline when movement felt like tipping over,

Stepping in a truck load of freshly harvested wheat, not understanding the dangers of a simple gesture,

Hearing a parent yell at a sibling with the wrong name till they got it right with a smirk on your face,

Those knowing looks between friends and buddies in planning the next escapade,

Sneaking back into the house at some ungodly hour, hoping all were asleep,

The moment in your brain when you heard your name being said from your parents' room,

The anxiety we put ourselves through when we were sneaking out and back in was worse than any punishment ever meted out.

Finding those hiding spots where we could be alone and not share everything.

Fighting with each other, as it was a way to get attention from everyone in the house.

Our first loves and the absolute certainty we wouldn't survive without them.

That first foray into discovering our sexuality and theirs, which we knew had consequences.

Buddying up to party the night away with the pure abandon of youth.

Turning around to find a parent there to drag your behind home before true trouble began.

The pranks we pulled and schemed on each other are still vivid in our hearts.

Learning how fast the vehicle would go in our invincibility of youth.

If we ever clocked the miles we walked while growing up and out it would be mind boggling.

Leaving the nest of growth to begin the next life cycle during higher education allowed those memories to settle.

We began to change what we would become but not who we are.

Sitting with new friends, old cronies, you once again live the memories, telling the stories.

You see the faces, hear the laughter, feel the growth, and know with certainty that you lived your life while growing.

Once in a while a memory will pop into your mind and you will remember a look of the purest love between your parents.

That is the memory when we truly feel great love and respect for the people that gave us all that we became.

Cherish the memories, share the story, and be you when passing them on to your family.

Lust

January 10, 2012

The ultimate peak of desire for some wanting . . .

Knowing the peak is sharp and pointed and has no place to stand,

It may balance for the seconds it takes to get past the peak and then it is gone.

The one-sidedness of lust is only there long enough to receive.

Seeing something that you want above all else is a headiness which has no comparison.

Intelligently we know that once we have it born of lust it means nothing.

It becomes an object or a person that has no appeal.

Understanding the feeling passes, we find ourselves lusting after other stuff.

It is meaningless if received, unless it is born of hard work and purpose.

The increase in blood flow in the body from lusting is not a bad thing.

It lets you know you are alive and want something, and it is up to you whether or not you pursue.

Healthy lust can be extremely funny if you see the humour in our lives.

Recognizing the feeling for exactly what it is keeps it healthy.

Life throws so many things in our path that we lust after which are out of our reach.

In the head of hearts we control those desires, as intelligent life should.

Why we lust after anything, as it is an empty emotion, is the question begging to be answered.

Laugh and cry knowing you feel intensely, and that you can be moved to that great intensity.

Life is short and we need to lust at living every moment to completeness.

Moonlight
January 10, 2012

The moonlight bounces off the frozen pond.

The edge of the pond reflects the small piles of winter's snowy cover.

The full moon is bright and has clarity in the atmosphere.

Stars that are close to the moon are so clear that you see red, white, and blue from refracted light.

The icy pond is dimpled while the wind blows it into frozen waves.

The sky is silent in the evening night.

The moon moves across the horizon and where sky meets earth it is a darker black.

The dry grass pokes through the snow in the pasture in winter's rest.

The snow crunches as the coyote makes its way to hunt for its very survival.

On a moonlight night there is something stunning about watching a herd of deer walk single file.

The moonbeam has changed its ripple of light in so short a time.

The stand of trees to the south of the pond is so stark, yet hides so much life.

With the moonlight, the bare and naked trees take on shadows of their own.

The moonbeam can touch so much of nature and our imaginations can soar.

With the moon sleeping away the daylight, we work at our tasks of survival.

As the moon is our nightlight, we appreciate all we are given and rest, knowing that we hunted another day and survived.

Sensuality

January 10, 2012

The invitation in sensuousness can be so subtle you don't
know it till you have stroked.

A few years of a slight sensuality to the continuous flirting,

The breathtaking smile on the corners of your mouth,

The slight twinkle in the depth of your eyes makes you
want to question what is hiding.

It is an understanding on levels that don't need explanation,
as you know how sensual it is,

An all-encompassing feel for the heart of the sensuality in
closeness.

The racing beat of hearts being in proximity to an aura in
purity,

It is the pheromones that are going ballistic when the sensu-
ous is close.

There is vividness in the touch of fingertips to any part of
the target,

A smile can share so much of the hidden duality to a per-
son's sensuality.

The colour in a person's eye can tell of so many moments
directed at someone who is beyond the logic of our need.

The laugh can be so fraught with sensual meaning you
could be surprised at how you feel.

Sensuality washes through your soul and body and euphoria
teases the edge of the thoughts.

Smells of sensuality can be so defined we don't even know what the scent is.

Sensuality can be just being in the same room as someone who wants to be there.

The air crackles and vibrates on levels so deep that it defies intelligence in feeling.

Sensuousness can be derived from the way you walk and the person viewing the strut,

A lift of the brow unconsciously when in direct context to another's sensuousness.

The smallest gesture of moistening the lips takes on a whole new meaning of sensuality.

The act of running our fingers through our hair can turn into a stroke of pure delight.

The one positive, absolute gesture of sensuous sensuality is in being yourself.

Only your true mate of mates will find you.

It is the sensuality of another's being that starts you on the path to loving unconditionally.

Purity
January 12, 2012

The innocence of a newborn child,

And the notes in the music that will make you cry.

The ring in a person's unexpected laugh,

And the fallen snow that blankets the earth.

The raindrop that falls on your face during a shower,

And the tear shed with grief and loss.

The touch to soothe another's hurt and pain,

And the smell of fresh baked goodness.

The love in someone's eyes without guile,

And the hug of contact for another life.

The steam infused in the air when stocking,

And the soft touch of fur of the dog curled in comfort.

The snore of your mate that lets you know you are not alone,

And the joy of arriving home to peace of heart.

The crispness in the bite of apple,

And the crunch of life when out for a walk.

The shimmering leaves on the trees before it rains,

And the tinkle of wind chimes that note the movement of air.

The clear taste of water when thirsty,

And the dirt in the spring warming from the sun.

The smells of life all around us,

And the beat of your heart when quietly resting.

The wrinkles on our faces that tell us we live,

And the family, whether we like them or not.

The friends that have been so much a part of us,

And the friends that are no longer with us but are missed.

The parents that gave us life and love,

And the ability to pass to our children the best of us.

The arms and heart to hold and cherish your life,

And the will to laugh at yourself and with others.

The tongue and lips to tell the world, life is worth living every moment,

And the grace and sense to be humble.

The gift of purity is in every one of us,

And the purity is in how we view and live our lives.

Angels

January 14, 2012

In the unexpected flash of light where there should be none,

The angel winked to bring awareness to your space.

They are the guidance when our lives seem troubled,

Air movement where there should be stillness,

Wrapping their auras around your soul so you feel at peace,

Gathering together the people you need here to help your
direction,

Opening your mind and heart to dream of desires once
wanted,

Recognizing the path of choice when so many are on your
map.

There was someone that left this world to protect you in this
one.

Sometimes they will actually put that earthly angel in your
path.

Being busier makes for unawareness in other crucial parts
of life.

The sense of the angel can put obstacles of many kinds in
your way, trying to slow down your speed.

A total lack of appreciation of living our lives is when our
heart of angels seems to disappear.

We think, we stop, and we smell the earth and the flowers,
the fruits of our labours.

We connect with others to share our bodies and our hearts
in happily ever after.

Our guides sit back in the recesses of our auras and gently poke and prod when we stray.

Being back on the path, we should question even more of our angels.

Your angel will let you know what you searched for while you strayed.

In your mind and your heart and soul, the angel has given you everything to make a choice,

As we know that when we make the incorrect choice life will happen.

We live our daily lives but we know something is missing.

The sense of guidance lets the straying begin again with the necessary obstacles of awareness.

The angels allow this pattern to happen repeatedly until we grasp the answer in who we are.

As we live our lives, we want to believe there is more than this.

We know heartbreaking sadness and devastating loss and mind-numbing boredom.

It is our choice in how we deal with all of these drastic changes in our possession.

Somewhere in all of this sits our guidance, and we still ignore the direction it shows us.

We need to feel to know we live and have respect for ourselves and the gift of us.

Ideas about what angels are and how we perceive the notion of help from a different plane other than the one we are on is a stretch even for the most educated mind.

Take a moment if you question the maps of your life and the pattern will emerge.

We only choose the small things, yet the map may tell you differently.

Realistically, maybe the angels are the lights at the intersections in the map of living.

As with anything in our lives, we know only where we began. We have been navigating the life map ever since and will continue.

Life is a series of unexpected turns, stops, slowing down, merges, potholes, and double lines of passing and moving forward.

It is the angels of the universe that decide when you have arrived.

Live your life proudly and live all angelic moments.

Decisions

January 17, 2012

Daily, we have choices to make and decisions to finalize.

In the choices we see and analyze and finally take the option we think of as certainty.

The outside influences get the information and then those decisions are forever locked to ours.

Our certainty must take every effort not to be thrown off course by doubt.

In our head there is never enough information to make a logical decision as we gather more.

The motivating factors in our options are the base of desires.

Deciding to live and feed ourselves and our family were the motivating bits of information in the immediate need.

The option of higher education came right along the time of understanding we are solely responsible for ourselves.

Choosing the education for the purpose of better quality of life was simple.

The decision to do this was only in the evening and living the necessity the other hours of life.

The years disappeared behind us as we opted to enhance our lives with things.

We have had it all, so to speak, along with the choices in our striving to achieve.

Somewhere in our achievements, love was the option that got destroyed.

Once it disappears we have the decision to make if it enhances or is a detriment to who we are.

Amazingly enough, the decision to choose to live without love brings a shocking amount of cynicism to our hearts.

Suddenly our lives are coloured by it, and when the gift is given and enjoyed the decision to live without it goes from bright to dark.

I have decided to choose the option of great love and the immense range of feeling.

A Word

January 21, 2012

A single word has suddenly been steeped with many meanings.

The word in any language is a beast, whether alone or in a pack.

The guidance from the word has pointed out the path that was once lost from itself.

The scent on the wind has been noticed along the time, but lost in movement.

Once in a while during times of rest and renewal the scent was caught and distance was lost from the word.

The affinity to be able to sit and write my heart has settled the urge to disappear.

The roaming desire has finally stopped pulling me away from the words.

I have arrived at my habitat where the word resided in its den and has marked my territory.

I can now sit at the base of my creativity and allow the river of words to flow.

There has been a torrent of words in the expanse of such short leading intensity.

When I fear my ability of creative energy, the word appears in my face in the most unexpected manner.

The word has been a person who has been there for years and didn't recognize the muse.

The word has been a picture and a natural draw to animal symbolism.

The word has been as simple as a sweet treat from another place.

The word has been a piece of prose rewritten by someone from an unknown author that has held my being for years.

The word is part of a gift of guidance to the culmination of my creative soul for others to know.

The word has been the alpha male in the pack inside my heart.

The word has been forcing itself to the forefront of my creative mind.

The word has emptied itself of all distractions and the scent has finally let the creative wanderer acknowledge its home.

When I feel the calmness of the word, I know the massive energy flowing beneath the surface.

I fall into that massive pit of blazing heat being generated and I feel the flow onto the page of prose.

At any time in my doubts of ability, I now understand the universe will throw that word at me when I need it most.

I am surrounded by the word in love, in pictures, in warm objects, in hard and malleable metal, and in my natural habitat of hearth and home.

Once upon a time, there was a storyteller who had a word as a muse . . .

Rules

January 25, 2012

A moment in a life that changes all the rules of a lifetime,

The risk taken in such a short period of that moment.

The processing of the information was supposed to be well thought of.

No notice was taken in seeing the players in the chance regular encounters.

Moments turned into years without acknowledgment of waves in emotion.

Reading the space of a smile in the absent-minded twinkle in the eye,

A sight of physical manifestation in appreciation of a well-developed specimen of masculinity,

The acknowledgment of the specimen in an offhand gesture.

Once out of sight, out of mind, and we see before us what we have.

It is the physical reminder of our choices of when we loved.

The rules of a lifetime were well on the way of changing how we view and think.

The idea of the viewpoint was truly foreign as we succumbed to the tangled emotion.

Hearts were at stake and we didn't really comprehend who it was that was pouring forth their heart.

Interpretation of the information was lost in translation temporarily.

The gift was truly given of the hearts, when realization hit, they finally joined their essence.

This has not been a choice of "If it is so, it just is."

As we look at our physical reminders of our choice, we comprehend the loss of love in its purest form.

There was no introduction to another's essence. It just was.

Patience was required, as an essence needed processing ability on the path which had been stepped into.

Tolerance has become the requirement for the other essence to guide it back to the love that had developed.

The rules of our lifetime have changed the essences irrevocably, just as they should.

Changes in us have happened no matter if we chose to stay with our physical reminders,

Human emotion and thought processes will always lead us back to our essences.

The essences have lived their lives by the rules as they were taught and ensconced in.

Only they know if they can shed the tarp of the rules that hold them under.

The hearts at stake may only get this purity in emotion this once, as they have spent their lives giving themselves to others.

Physical reminders will not understand the balm in each other's arms they have found to making them whole again.

Abandon

January 31, 2012

A loss of a promise once whispered in action,

Intentioned or not, the loss is no less felt.

The illusion of the gain in our daily routine,

Buried so deep in our lives, is our reaction.

Blindly we go about living and putting all things in order.

Substance becomes the eating routine in discovery.

Dusting the household in trying to remove the film of
smothering;

Scrubbing the floor involves the release of pent up, useless
energy.

Dishes clang against one another in hopes of hearing.

A simple change of the bedding removes hidden creases.

There is intermittent sleeping as your body knows your
reactions.

We do mindless tasks to cope with the changes in our
beings.

Our brains keep us on the straight and narrow, no matter
what.

Beating on the rugs to remove the dust and grime from be-
ing walked on,

We don't get all of the dirt out when beating vigorously.

Our tasks of the day are only the visual result of what has
been accomplished.

Payment of those tasks may be monetary and enhance our
lifestyle.

They give every day a reason to arise and a direction to focus on.

The foundations you build with others become an integral part of your life.

When parts of the base root are ripped from the whole, changes are immediate.

It is the steadiness of those tasks that help our coping mechanisms.

Once acceptance becomes part of the actions to feeling, the loss in change is easier.

We all hope against hope that the intensity we know will be there and not change.

The feeling of abandonment cuts so deeply we weep without knowing.

We do by rote, as this has been the steadfastness in living.

In each and every one of us we abandon some small piece of what we were.

There are different degrees of abandonment and every degree is steeped in pain.

Whether we weep in tears or in self-preservation, we acknowledge the abandonment of what was to what is.

This is no less simple than living every moment to its conclusion and knowing you did this with abandon.

Abandon our restrictions, as we have been taught limitations within the values of this life.

A Question

January 31, 2012

When you looked, did you see
Into the heart of me?
When you moved to touch,
Did you feel how much?
When you breathed the air around,
Did the scent abound?
When we greeted,
Did you know what I needed?
When our paths crossed,
Did you know about my pending loss?
When we regularly met,
Did you know the time was not yet?
When your eyes twinkled in my sight,
Did you know it would take all your might?
When you laughed at all the wit,
Did you know I would fit?
When you finally held me against your all,
Did you know I felt so small?
When you see me now,
Do you ask yourself, "How?"
When I sit and think,
I am aware you could be gone in a blink.

When the thought of you is strong,
I don't question if it's wrong.
When my life finally noticed you were missing,
I knew I could do no resisting.
When my day is full of fear and strife,
I cherish you in my life.
When my feet hit the floor,
I know you are out my door.
When I see the mirror of your eyes,
I have to believe there are no lies.
When the look of love shines from my face,
I have to know it has found its place.
When my head overrides my heart with doubt,
I picture you with all the clout.
Life gave us this love untended,
Forever in our hearts to be mended!

Guilt

January 31, 2012

Staring out of my window at the naked trees of winter,

It has become a stark reminder that the fall of my life is in full swing.

During the spring, we are full of promise and know all.

We argued with those in the winter of their knowledge.

They know so little of what we can relate to. That it is our ignorance.

The ones that are wintering in the spring and summers of their lives make you open to old ideas.

In the late summer of my being, our lives changed drastically.

Suddenly, winter was thrust upon the summer to end it prematurely.

I never imagined my summer would end so abruptly.

My fall began in choices of why, what, where, and when.

The leaves were raked into piles around my emotions.

When all were bagged and ready for burning, the bag split.

The leaves swirled around my life and I had to face the autumn before I could face winter.

In facing the leaves of my emotions I fell into a pile that nearly choked my heart.

I came up for air in the crispness to know my fall was just beginning.

The winter in my fall is moving farther away as I accept ice-melting warmth from another fall.

A rain of tears have flowed from late summer to now.

The cloud of guilt is beginning to slow the rain to a light drizzle.

Banks have been crested many times and the river has ebbed to where it started.

The guilt the fall has carried forth needs to be skipped across the river and let alone.

The winter's conclusion will be the same no matter what the fall does.

The fires in fall burn hot and the embers never truly go cold.

It will only take the smallest breeze to breathe the fire to life.

Embers have the smallest amount of smoke and the most enduring amount of heat.

My fall is in full swing and I need to smell and see the changes without any guilt.

Terrors

February 7, 2012

Out of nowhere comes the vibrating sensation of a train
bearing down on you.

You move to get out of its way but when you look you see
lights.

Closing your eyes only intensifies the need to flee.

In the choking feeling, the reaction is the tears beginning to
roll.

It releases some of the horror as you sense things are out of
control.

No matter how you think, the terror in the pit of your stom-
ach it still is there.

It freezes you in a spot and walking and moving doesn't
move you.

Opening your eyes only confirms you ate and swallowed the
terror.

Until you move away from yourself and the indulgence in
feeling the vibration, you don't escape.

The train of emotion just keeps bearing down on you with
no relief.

Moving away from the train of terror is only delaying the
inevitable wreck.

When it happens all you can do is let it run over you and
hope it doesn't totally tear you apart.

By the time the caboose is finished, the terrors have
changed into acceptable portions.

One portion at a time isn't simple, but it gives you an opportunity to analyze and digest the emotional terror.

As you stand and watch the train disappear in your life, all you really feel is an emptiness of cleansing.

Somewhere in you an understanding begins to show itself—that you have grown in your life.

This growth shows your ability to deal with real and imagined terrors and still be whole.

Waiting II
February 9, 2012

We go through our lives having the sense that not all is fulfilled.

This sense we have, began at a very young age.

This sense should really be the seventh sense in the human condition.

The monetary amount of funds and time in education, families, and economic gain are truly astronomical.

There is no science to this sense, as you cannot use the other capabilities to pinpoint where it comes from and where it goes.

It feels like a cloak that never is satisfied, no matter your actions or lack thereof.

We look to other people and things to strip that sensation from us.

The humanity requires the physical evidence to believe what is not there, but felt and endured.

Absent-minded behaviour (or what seems like that) is what it is.

Look closer, you will see the person watching to see what happens as a direct result of the action.

Our work is an extremely good example of this sense.

We act out the requirements of our employment while we wait for the monetary gain.

We give and raise our children to the best of our ability while we wait for them to grow.

We give attention and actions to our life's mate while we wait to see if any pleasure is going to be reacted upon.

If the action has no reaction it intensifies the sense of waiting.

Inaction is waiting in its truest form, yet all actions result in the same form.

Analyzing behaviour, words, actions, life, circumstance, coincidence, and choices will result in exactly the same sense that has yet to be labeled but is just as real.

When you sit and listen to the views and thoughts of another person you are waiting to sense the result.

Smiling and laughing will result in others doing exactly the same, as it is a pleasurable action.

We wait while living our actions and inactions and interacting with others.

Time is not the sense of awareness and it is not the sense of waiting.

Time may heal all wounds (or most of them), yet it is not time. It is the waiting.

It has been time that has made me aware of this sense, and the urge to act in some way, shape, or form.

This unnamed sense has been thrust into my meagre life and forever changed the ledge feeling.

Sometimes the description has been "waiting for the other shoe to drop."

What happened with the first shoe when waiting?

One innocuous incident while someone was waiting for the reaction.

The future will unfold as it is supposed to and awareness will be prevalent.

The waiting continues while we live, breathe, eat, sleep, and be.

We interact with our fellow beings while waiting for the one sensation that seems to temper the waiting sense.

When great love becomes a part of our lives it seems to push the waiting sense into the background.

As with all things, changes are part of humanity.

Awareness with stunning clarity is this sense that doesn't change. Life is the wait.

A Number

February 19, 2012

A number has become so intrinsic in my life.

It is a shadow that sits on the edge of my senses.

Throughout my life the number has great significance.

Lucky thirteen in order of my birth.

A couple of my choices of love or insanity have had their birthdates on the thirteenth.

A choice of love that lasted for a number of years has been marked in ending on the thirteenth.

The number has followed me all my life in good choices and bad.

The number has not been unlucky for me, as I have been blessed every day.

A number has caused a great deal of surrealism in my life.

I have pushed the number and the only thing that was unlucky was that it should not have happened in the first place.

All the hindsight in the world would not change the number in my life.

It is my order as well as the hilarity of how bizarrely it has played a role in my life.

The universe may have played no part of the scenery in my living, but it has kept my sense of humour intact.

The first choice was May thirteenth, and again, no error as my son arrived from this choice.

The second choice was October thirteenth, and my own blind insanity carried forth this one.

This one took the universe literally and pushed my energies sense of humour.

He was thirteen years older.

We married on October thirteenth.

There were thirteen steps.

We married at the thirteenth hour.

We said "I do" at thirteen minutes after.

He had thirteen cents in his pocket.

There were thirteen people at the ceremony.

I pushed the boundaries and the result was a life lesson in insanity—mine.

I should have known better, as the universe has taught me over the years

To stop messing with what you are supposed to do and follow only your heart.

I try not to be obtuse but as I write this I see how wrong I have been.

I have given and lost yet still held on to the part of me that makes it all worthwhile.

Me, and my lucky thirteen.

Smoking
February 22, 2012

.A year ago I made a choice to end a long standing behav-
iour.

A desire to be out from under the urge to poison myself.

A book held the key to putting the addiction in perspective,

An addiction that was expensive and not pleasurable.

Years of feeding the desire to continuously feel the raw
hunger for the tube of tobacco and nicotine.

The option of quitting caused a great deal of nausea and
pure fear.

Idly picking up the book and pursuing one more expert on
the subject,

The read hooked me on the first page and I wanted to read
more.

The book disappeared at the same time my friend returned
to Calgary.

It left the need to read more of this man's insight.

The book was never far from my thoughts.

I knew within a few days that I needed to read the book as
much as to reach for the nicotine.

In the book store the clerk couldn't find it on the shelf yet
the book was in inventory.

I was bordering almost on panic at the thought of leaving
without that purchase.

Someone walked by and heard the exchange and informed
the clerk it was still packed.

I was waiting for the book and the panic abated, knowing I would have it.

My true desire to be able to possibly break the addiction was uplifting.

The road ahead to being nicotine free was finally visualized.

The path told me to continue until the body and mind absorbed the truth about the greasy black friend.

I read, I thought, I read, I fought, and I read again.

The nicotine craving won out at the end of the read.

I let the book fall open and read from there for more insight.

I finished the read again and was still not sure what I wanted to do.

Upon running out of the nicotine fix, the purchase was simple.

It was a process I had done a couple of times a week for years.

This time the mind and body heard the monetary price.

The brain was finally and truly appalled at the monetary price of craving nicotine.

The vow was made that that would be the final price paid.

It has been and my awareness is daily that I can survive in my life without my greasy black friend.

It never stopped me from living, but now I am free.

Growth

February 26, 2012

Lying under the oak tree in a copse of cedars in my youth,

I watched the sunlight dapple the ground around me as I lay there wondering,

What did my life have in store for me?

The light played colours you could only see when you let yourself be.

The peace of quiet enveloped my surging mind, just to rest.

A part of me always looked for the lone pattern Mother Nature gave us to discover.

I could feel the ants and bugs crawl over me, as I was in their way.

The feeling of other life and creatures that serve some purpose didn't register when I wandered in my mind.

There was no feeling or sense of my life slipping away, as I was only beginning my journey.

On levels I am not even sure I understand or comprehend, the lone oak tree and my spot has been my sanity.

There was substance on my walk to that special spot and when in season two rocks opened the hickory nut.

When I took the way of the field, the blossoms of alfalfa were suckled for their honey.

The stroll to the spot was never hurried, as I felt every step and knew there was quiet of mind.

My life has taken its many twists and turns, yet when life is overwhelming I can find the quietness of the lone oak tree.

It has been my haven in my soul when I needed it most, and when I reach it through my life, the quiet is still achieved.

Now the stroll through my mind to that spot may take longer, as the fields have gotten rockier and the animal holes have gotten deeper.

The navigation of the fields, lanes, and the substance taken along the way, make me smile.

The blessing of my son and the joy of respect—he is strong and loving, in spite of the stumbles as a mother.

The lone oak tree and my spot underneath have never been about better times.

In some ways that spot taught me I would need to be a tough nut to crack.

The last couple years of anxiety, hurt, loss, pain, loss of sense of direction, and a loss of my sense of me.

I am fully aware of the boulders I am floundering against and maneuvering around, and along the way was the healing process.

I am picking myself up from the ground and shaking off the bugs and the dirt and scattering them in all directions.

My lone oak tree and my spot will always be there in my being when next I need a quiet rest.

The direction I follow has finally been cleared and this path through the field must be enjoyed as I discover the words.

Flashes

February 27, 2012

In a moment you are there building the fire of intensity.

It comes so quickly it is upon us before we are totally aware.

There is no gentle heat but an intense, all-consuming heat.

It is felt in every nerve in your body, right down to the tips of your fingers.

The tingling and burning go through the bloodstream until you begin to sweat.

An all over warmth flashes through our senses and takes an immediate toll.

A thin piece of gauze can feel heavy and constraining in those flashes.

Clothing cannot be removed fast enough to cool the skin and feel some relief.

The flashes come and go at will and no pattern emerges, for every woman is different.

The blatant stage of a woman's life is definitely not an enjoyed aging process.

Some of us feel the trigger can be something consumed, like sugar.

Chocolate can be the pitfall for another woman.

The time of day can be when the body decides it needs to apply the flash of heat.

Those flashes can be a couple of minutes or they can continue for hours.

Night can be the worst time of the twenty-four hours, as they seem to be more intense.

The amount of sweat that is soaking the clothing and bedding—there should be tonnes lost.

It is not enough that we bear the children and the intense pain that is part of womanhood.

We endure the cleansing of our blood on a regular basis and the pain associated with that.

The flashing heat we begin to endure in the truly mature years borders on a bad joke.

As with all of our lives, we have endured what makes women unique.

The menopausal state that we go into at this stage of our aging should be a pleasure, not more endurance.

This marks the end of the pain-filled child bearing years to the younger women that are filled with ideals of the joy of procreation.

As I find myself enduring the flashing heat and all that goes with this process,

I look forward to those flashes ending as the cleansing of my aging happens.

This life I live and have endured at times has been interesting and I am happy to live with the flashes.

These flashes unite the mature women of the world who have contributed so much, to so many lives.

As one of these women I have noticed all about my life has become as intense as those flashes of heat.

Lies

March 1, 2012

Is there pain when your jaw moves involuntarily when you
think of lying?

Are you lying to the universe, your life, your wife, and the
one that hurts the most—yourself?

The length of time it happens tells you when last you faced
you.

When questions are asked do you require the time for make
believe?

Is the truth still a viable part of your being or has it been
lost forever?

The lie you have lived all your life has come full circle and
your option is correction or continuance.

Happiness of heart has finally touched your life for you to
grasp and cherish.

The layering of the lie continuously told by you to salve
whom you are has been the obligation and honour.

The first lie is also the last lie, as everything in between is
the pain and the loss of love and trust.

Is recognition of true emotion when it arrives accepted for
the truth or turned into a lie?

The levels of emotion are what trigger the desire to have
what is given finally, in love.

Pulling on ourselves in a direction that is truly foreign to
our beings is what causes the devastation.

Being true to the truth is what requires the constant dili-
gence.

The lies from another are questioned or accepted as reality.

Varying degrees of lying to protect another are still lies, even when the lies are only to protect yourself from dealing with the truth.

Little white lies, big fat lies, the mother of all lies, the fantasy lie, the reality lie, the omission lie—all have the same result.

They cause hurt, anger, and stress that we are inundated with daily.

Is the lie to one and not the other, or does the lie splatter all in its wake?

The lie teaches all in your life to accept what they see and not what is the foundation of the observed actions.

We teach our children to lie and accept less as adults when they only see the lie.

Once in a while the people we love the most are the ones that have the ability to see the truth beneath the lie.

Protecting the initial lie with more lies and then living that reality means you have wrought more to repair.

Success in life happens with honest hard work and dealing with glitches as they happen.

The working harder does not guarantee more success or more money, or more prestige.

It does allow more freedom to grow our success, to eat better, to drive newer, to travel more, and to leave more behind for our children.

Our changes in our growth do not negate the lies told along the way unless you stopped long enough to change the reality.

When we turn around and see the path we have travelled and the lies told along the way, are we certain of who we are?

Had the truth been told along the way, how different would our lives have been? Or maybe not?

At the end of our day, if we visit with ourselves just for a few moments, would we be honest with ourselves or do we continue to live in the pretense of truth?

The heart of us is the truth and it is the heart that keeps it safe.

The lie is the head, as it justifies the lie and behaviours.

Landscapes

March 3, 2012

Our views have changed as drastically as the landscape has
been stripped.

The scrub, the trees, and the overgrown dead grass and
weeds are being pushed and pulled apart.

It has been piled into a windrow to be disposed of when
time allows.

The roots that have kept everything strong and in place are
being cut up and ground back to earth.

The windrows will decay in the place where pushed, as the
moisture and nutrients replenish the soil and the life un-
seen.

The tidiness of the windrows shows the tidiness of the
owner operating the bulldozer.

A quarter has been made ready to plant a new crop to en-
hance his standing within himself to leave a legacy for
the next generation.

He will reap the rewards of the many hours of work and
hiding he has done for lofty ideals.

His progeny may appreciate the time he took from his life
to ultimately improve theirs.

There is no guarantee that they will, as they have not put
the effort into stripping the naked hard brush on the land.

Where once there was scrub, trees, weeds, marsh grass, and
wildlife that roamed the habitat,

There are now many fields of flat, clear land and hills that
await the equipment that begins a new season of growth
and change.

The human beast upon the mechanical beast has forever
changed the landscape on this section.

In a very short period of time I have had the honour or hor-
ror of seeing the changing landscape on Mother Earth,
and our hearts and lives.

Honour that Mother Earth has given us the ability to choose
our livelihoods and our choices of what we do with the
gifts.

Horror as I watch, see, and find myself in the middle of op-
posing forces and abilities in our lives.

Insight into who and what I am has changed my landscape
as I live, while another dies.

This may be the choice of my life, to pursue my heart and
my desire in truly discovering who I am.

The heart of me is held in another's heart, and acknowledg-
ing the changing landscape is easier than accepting the
heart.

The generation that he changed the landscape for will never
understand the cost and the choices,

The cost of ensuring his being is the last thing of impor-
tance in his life, as this is the way he lives.

The importance has been his children and the blessings they
are.

Showing and teaching the children are of paramount desire
for him in his life lessons to them.

Looking upon the section of landscape, you know how he
lived his life, raised his children, made his choice of
spouse, and his view of himself.

All things neat and tidy in his head, but not necessarily in
his environment.

All things are neatly lined up on the shelf of his life, from
the scrub of their births to exacting windrows that he

keeps trying to bulldoze into place when the brush just wants to run rampant for a while.

The landscape is so entrenched in you that understanding the landscape needs to change for planting the seeds of the next generation,

Changing your landscape is the true horror for you, as you immediately dove into the forest at the overwhelming love you felt for another.

As her landscape changed and the seed took hold to grow into loving you as you have always wanted,

Bulldoze your landscape all you want. Pile dirt on top of your love.

This landscape you can't change, as it isn't yours to change but accept as given.

Challenges
March 11, 2012

The first step in the morning can be the longest step of the day.

The foot slipped on the shiny side of my mourning.

Teetering on the balls of my feet I balanced the emotion for a little while.

My domain got cleaner as the wavering became more intense.

Gingerly moving forward into the unplanned foray of desolation, things were put in place.

Turning around to begin the walk of the day the emotional starvation rose to my throat.

Music held no distraction, as the steps were not fast enough to avoid the trigger of emotion.

It landed in my core and ripped through me before I could grip the desolation.

The challenge seems to be daily as I step, one at a time.

The next step will be into a free fall down the slope to the pits of desolation.

The footholds on the climb back out are tenuous at best.

When the edge of the slope is close and it requires the last difficult push, emotion gives way and I have returned to the bottom once again.

Some days the challenge becomes not dealing with the roller coaster from emotional oblivion.

The days when the aloneness of my journey takes hold I reach out to my trusted group.

They listen and try to comprehend the shouting I am doing at the bottom of the pit.

They hear what I am saying but know there is no rope ladder of understanding that can be thrown.

I let the tears flow, as the challenge of trying to stop them is pointless.

Sitting at the bottom of the slope, looking for the direction of healing—it seems so faint.

I can walk the pit from beginning to end but until I look past the spot in front of me, I am stuck.

The direction is not right or left, or up and down, but inwards to my heart.

Challenging my head to stay focused on here and now is difficult, as in the future things need to be done.

I only have the present, and so do my support people, and sometimes in the bottom of the pit I reach high enough to give something back.

As I climb out once again into my living, I am aware that depression peeks around the corner of my emotions.

My challenge is the awareness of the pit of dark emotion that I must negotiate around for my health.

I survived another slippery slope.

The Gift

March 18, 2012

Reality seems so simple in its complicated manner.

We do what is necessary in our routines without specific thought.

It is movement of our energies to complete the tasks of life.

We plan and pay for our homes and we accumulate important stuff.

All is well in our environment and occasionally we are more thankful than others for our sanity, home, and stuff.

If we are lucky enough, we have friends and family, neighbours and cronies to keep our lives interesting.

We engage the humanity pool to find our mate for life.

Some of us have had to throw them back and choose again.

Hope against hope we choose wiser the next time and that all is well.

As we live we discover that the choice isn't perfect but it is better than the previous choices.

Some of us have been chasing the humanity pool in our heads too long.

Years pass with the pick and while not perfect, it is good.

Personalities clash and ideas are let go and you live.

We get to know that there are people that chose from the humanity pool and know they chose wrong, but picture the art, rather than the pain.

I swear humanity has a short-circuited brain that masquerades the intelligence arriving from our hearts.

It is the emotion that orders our heads to think a certain way, and when we watch that we see.

One day our orderly life is disrupted in the most painful way possible, with death and dying.

It is not the death that is difficult to cope with—it is the dying of the connected family.

Swift release of death may be painful and devastating, but it is much easier accepted.

Watching a spouse disappear a little at a time tears a part of you to shreds.

One small part of the personality disappears with the onset of progression.

We question them and the response is nothing. The medical field sometimes only hinders finding the cause.

We push for help and understanding while we watch them leave in bits and pieces.

When help arrives, the diagnosis is made and we are so unprepared for the information.

Denial is the first and foremost response to listening to the information being simulated by our hearts and bodies.

Acceptance is a long way off and the path you traverse on your way is terrifying.

Higher intelligence may listen but have no comprehension of the emotion, as there is no evidence to support it.

The people left behind to mourn the life that is still living are well aware of the losses.

We master the path we are on in hopes of keeping our health and abilities in check.

We reach out to the masses in hopes they can give us a positive manner in which to cope.

When all else fails we weep for loss, for guidance, for friendship, for family, for ending the emotional upheaval we find ourselves in.

We choose to do the things that will look after the person with the illness and pray for strength.

The hoops are put in place to jump through when figuring out all of the mechanics.

I have learned that the hoops can be the distraction for coping with life's immediate changes.

A step away from the middle of the upheaval gives you a chance to breathe and view from a different angle.

The difficult choices still need to be made but you feel a little better prepared.

There is no one out there that can make your choices when the decision is yours.

You choose when all information settles in your heart and brain.

It is sobering in all ways when you have to choose for someone who no longer can.

I had the required desires from the spouse to know without doubt what he wanted.

A person that is terminally ill with vascular dementia may not always recognize or know you.

The question is always there if they still know you loved them and that they were an integral part of your life.

When my options were spread in front of me about care for him, he voiced again what he wanted.

His eyes and voice told me that he knew I would follow through on his wishes.

He said his final goodbye to me and calmed my emotional being.

The gift he gave me was "Thank you, live your life, you have the freedom to do so."

In the process I questioned if I made a difference in anyone's life.

The gift from my spouse told me in many ways that I have. I have finally arrived at emotional peace and the gift was the catalyst to acceptance.

Away

March 26, 2012

We know the destination when we leave the immediate vicinity.

We know how long we are going to be away.

We know how we will travel to the place of our choice.

We know who we are going to be with while away.

We know the plan of arrival and departure.

We believe we know the reason we are going away.

We believe it is to get away from our routines and a gift to someone else of a memory.

We see the sights and attractions, the pictures taken, and the memories are stored away.

We lie down at night and relive the sights and sounds, the pleasure and irritations.

We then realize that it is only a place in the world to land and see.

We continue to think of our realities back where we began and parts of us yearn for that peace of place.

When we are away from what grounds us, we feel intensely uneasy.

We are fully aware of the stress associated with being in a place that offers no comfort.

When life is overwhelming my being, I crave the grounding of my very small piece of life I have.

When away from my life I have, it gives me a chance to take stock of the life I lead.

The distance away should be comprehension of all you are.

When away, we believe it will change the perspective.

When away, it only changes the time frame to deal with you.

Being away from the routines and painful presences only delays and hides the moments of decisions.

Being away is sometimes the only way of coping with drastic changes and challenges in our lives.

Life happens when here. Going away and returning is acceptance of how good life truly is.

Anywhere
April 4, 2012

The rumble of the plane as it jettisons down the runway for
takeoff to a destination of anywhere but here—

The rumble stops as the plane lifts off and I feel the
tears push out past my lids as part of me wants to stay
grounded and hide.

The weightless feeling is almost joyful as it lightens the
heaviness of sorrow I have been in for a while now.

Nowhere is far enough or close enough to release some of
the pent up hurt and frustration, the loss of all and gain
of everything.

There was no comprehension of that simple nuance and
now I am in the middle of it.

I am living it and so much emotion is tied directly to the
feeling.

I am leaving the place of tension and devastation and head-
ing directly back to where I began fifty-something years
ago.

I am only visiting once again to the root of what and who I
became.

No one is ever prepared for the life they lead and the deci-
sions they make when necessary.

We can have ideals about what we would do in that situa-
tion.

We would be so wrong on so many levels that it would sin-
gle-handedly blow your mind how far off you would be.

As the plane heads into the sunrise so does my hope that
with this visit some calmness will return to my heart.

In some ways this would be so much simpler if I could truly nail down the nausea and the uneasiness of all this.

I have stretched out the part of me that needs to be strong for me and for all others that are part of my life.

The one responsibility that I did and took on is the one causing the nausea of loss.

I am not getting my head and heart around the open wound that quiets. Then a phone call comes and it begins oozing poison again.

I feel I am drying up with the amount of tears I have cried, and then it begins again.

It is such devastating emotion that it has figuratively brought me to my knees on more than one occasion.

Letting go seems to be the most difficult thing to do, as it is hard to label the range of feeling there is.

I have spoken with the people that started the journey of maturity, motherhood—woman, wife, and true adult—with all the consequences and life.

It is with sadness that a grandmother will be no longer with us. My son and her children will miss her.

My thanks needed to be said at this time of my life, as the changes have taken hold and I have an appreciation of what was; what is.

I see the generations in each other and they will live on with my son.

My path of thanks is as complete as I need it to be for this part of anywhere.

Thanks to other friends and family that have taken my pro-verbial hand and just held me in place.

A few more days and I will listen to the rumble of the plane returning me to continuing my life that is full, and with so many more journeys to take.

Family Meal

April 7, 2012

As we gather around the breakfast table in the pleasure and
company of family,

There is laughter and fun with family that gets together
once in a blue moon.

There are favourite friends, favourite family, and wonderful
chats and jokes.

The time of Easter should be about space and living the
friendship entwined in the genes.

The restaurant has the buzz of busy and it is a special mo-
ment in our lives.

As the heartfelt laughter rings out for all to hear, you be-
lieve in family.

There are a few of us gathered in remembrance and with
new memories to hold and share.

When I look into the mirror of brothers there is no denying
the roots of the tree,

The influences of Mom and Dad and the fun in the simple
acts of our lives.

The memories flow with ease and any hurt and pain is left
behind in our maturity.

There is a closeness that was built directly by Mom.

It is felt as much today as it was when we all joined in cel-
ebration at those reunions as we grew.

The genes which course through every one of us make the
statement "The rooting was strong."

There are family pictures and when looking at these we
do remember those times and realize how we grew and
changed.

The sense of family was an idea Mom cultivated in every
one of us.

Surprising enough that sense still is strong today in us, yet
we let our busy lives get in the way of the effort required
to stay in touch.

In time the immediate brothers and sisters dwindle and still
the family gets larger.

We resemble our ancestors and the future generations will
resemble us now.

As a group over a meal there is a slight sadness that escapes
and washes over us as the time comes for an end to this
meal.

We know there will be another group with a different mix
and the laughter and fun will be just as intense.

I know the immediate family of my son is so small, yet the
intensity of family is cultivated in him.

It is joy, sadness, memories, life, and a love for family that
was passed directly from Mom and Dad in actions.

It was always the laughter in the end that was the loudest
noise in our home and still is today when together in
family.

Right Things
April 18, 2012

Returning to my life from anywhere has once again brought me face to face with my heart.

Upon looking at who I have become in the recent past, it begins to forge itself in me.

The mirror of your heart will reflect back what the image is and always has been.

Returning from anywhere has been one of my most enlightening experiences.

Realization of the pretenses lived and the lies told to the world, even when not necessary,

This has reinforced in me the desire to live my life and heart with honesty and who I am.

I have always tried to be who I am with integrity every day.

When I have slipped and tripped in my life, the message from my heart yells.

I eventually listen to the screaming going on in me and then I shut the brain off and hear with the truth of the heart.

Then and only then do I begin to correct the path that I am on and my being again comes to peace.

The most difficult part of knowing why the heart is hurt is knowing that my head allowed me to stray from my spirit.

When I stand in front of the aura that I find my heart has reached, all in me knows what must be done.

Somewhere in me that aura has reached into my life and shown me that the heart understands unwitting love.

It is not about planning, the pursuit, desire, or the range of human emotions.

It is about the spirituality of a love across the ages, that there is no comprehension in our realities.

Anywhere has taught me that humanity finds it easier to live in the lie than in their hearts.

Once I railed on the lie I found myself in, the rest was simple to understand: the right thing.

I am trying to walk away from my heart that has been grasped by another.

I am viewing my life from the inside out and trying to live by the right thing, no matter the hurt I feel.

The reality is that I have to do the right thing constantly so that the mirror image stays true.

The trip to anywhere has brought me home to my heart, my soul and being.

The right thing causes others pain as well. Are they doing the right thing for their hearts?

A Poem (Question II)
April 27, 2012

Is doing my right thing?
So ingrained it has a true ring.
How did you know?
I had no choice to let you go.
How do I stop the river of tears?
When I feel enveloped by my fears,
How do I see you without any pain?
When in my heart I feel the love we gained.
How do we maintain the connection?
As the universe kicks our foundations in elation,
How does the timbre in our voices?
Soothe so completely during our solstices.
How do we look upon our feet?
And walk away from the meet.
How do we gaze upon our hands in gift?
When all we want is to be left without a rift.
When entwined with our fingers,
All I know is I want to linger.
When in the hug, fit and tight,
We feel the joy and anxiety of our plight.
When my patience has run extremely thin,
You hold me in place till I grin.
When I strike out at the seeming injustices of living,

You let me go, as you know my heart is giving.
As I go through my daily life,
I am well aware you live as man and wife.
There is no anger towards how and when we met,
When will the universe show you how to let?
As we follow the path we are being guided down,
We hide our truth from possible talk around the town.
When our lives finally join the journey without the shame,
It is when the truth of love will shine without the game.
The sights and sounds of the daily grind,
Once in a while make us blind.
The life we live and see,
Is not really sometimes the best of you and me.
A gift was given in a dime,
During this turmoil in my time,
The wounds of love are being mined,
As told with love in this short rhyme.
Can our love survive and not be lost?
As we try and reduce the cost.
Wherever you are in our day,
You know my promise of love will stay.
When in proximity to the aura,
It seems the beauty is steeped in flora.
When at the end of our daylight,
I know my head and heart whisper goodnight,
A poem (Question III), will be finished when the time is
   right!

Arrogance
April 28, 2012

When there is no other around to keep the feeling in check,

It is a belief that can be so subtle as to not be noticed.

It is not specific to man or woman, as both can be simply arrogant.

The emotion of ego can override our sensibilities with the slightest ease.

We may think we have no arrogance, but it lies in all of us.

When we unconsciously judge another in comment or look,

Certainty can bring the feeling to the surface.

As patterns develop through our lives and things become stagnant, arrogance creeps in.

Suddenly when we look, things have stopped in an unfamiliar place.

Assumption becomes the life in the living space.

In our arrogance we continued to live as we have without care for ourselves and our mates.

When did the little things stop happening, and do we ask why we let them?

In hearing something so often, the arrogance appears in that we don't need to do anything because the ego has been engorged.

In some ways, isn't that the end of the marriage, when both have become so arrogant in their belief of certainty about their spouse?

How many times do we tune out the words and actions because of our arrogance?

We all change and in doing so we have to face our arrogant egos.

When facing them directly they can hurt you deeply, as you hurt others in it.

Arrogance is inbred in every one of us, as this is what motivates our brain to achievements.

As we grow into our age, does wisdom become the arrogance of survival and knowledge?

When we pass our knowledge to our children, does it come across to them as arrogance and that is why we believe they are not hearing excellent information?

Is their own arrogance in growing and maturing what irritates the parent from their creations?

We send our children into the world with considerable arrogance, that we have given them the best of hearth and home.

As we guide our lives through living and pass forth information that is helpful we believe we give our children better than the arrogance of the parents.

In our arrogance we missed the one most important element to ensure a well-rounded next generation:

The brutal arrogance of truth.

Everyone's truth can be very different, and when we can truthfully say, "I don't know, but I am willing to learn," then the arrogance is reduced to humanity.

My truth is exactly that, and in my own moments of arrogance I need to remember that.

When willing to learn, we absorb the information and put it to positive use and pass it to all whom are willing to learn with arrogance.

Our opinions are our arrogance.

The Dog's Day
May 2, 2012

A day like no other, yet like so many others.

Elation in arising to a pretty morning and filled with promise.

Thoughts run rampant as I go about my productive day.

People I spoke to gave me feedback that something I said along the way made a positive impact.

Once in a while I hear from those people and it does my soul good that I did positive things.

Today was a day when an animal taught me a lesson in my own humanity.

My own amount of emotional pain sometimes has consumed me to rivers of tears.

I have tried to put those feelings in perspective and it is extremely difficult at times.

As life does once in a while, it will center your attention around an event which didn't start that way.

It was just an old dog that shouldn't have been there.

We walked by the dog with minimal amount of thought and questioned who owned this animal.

As the day wore on and business happened, the dog became part of my line of sight.

It was when I stopped and watched that the pain was evident.

I wondered who the owner was, and they were cruel not to be watchful of their dog.

It became rapidly apparent to me how my fellow persons perceived that animal and my own sensibilities.

It brought tears to my eyes and heart when a simple gesture caused so much pain to the dog.

There was no gentleness in the gesture, just the business of living.

The dog was in obvious pain from old age and it pulled at my own kindness.

Why are we so cruel to an animal when the gesture of putting it to sleep would have been the kindest thing to do?

There is extreme pain when making those tough decisions and I am in the process of living it.

I cried for the pain the dog was in, and for my own pain of being alone as I watch the life leave my spouse.

I cried for the inhumanity of our intelligence, that we let life suffer in all forms for our so-called consciousness for other life.

In crying for that dog and so many other things, I understood people's need to hide for themselves.

When watching any life in pain and hurt we want to protect ourselves from those emotions, as there might be tough decisions that need to be made.

I am not ashamed to cry for that dog or my own pain (and someone else's), as I know I grow from feeling.

I have followed my heart in trying to get help for that animal and that is all that I can do.

My lesson by the end of the day and my tears have been I am thankful for what I have and who I am in all my emotions.

This day has confirmed my ability to see and feel another's life with compassion and empathy.

Adaptation

May 6, 2012

The turmoil in my heart continues to pull me in directions I was unaware of.

It is difficult to put the turmoil in the perspective where I am capable of dealing with the angst.

When I am relatively sure I have a handle on the changes within me, a trigger goes off and I am aching again.

My inner person sits on the edge of my turmoil and I feel the "I am right here."

When I reach out to grab me, it slips away as I touch the edge.

I am so entrenched in my being, my person keeps tripping me.

The changes that have happened to my external life are wreaking havoc with my internal person.

The internal me is screaming at the top of my lungs to let go of the external changes.

The external changes will continue to happen, and with that, your growth.

I have lived a certain way my whole life and letting her go to the wind is painful.

She defined who she was, how she thought, what she believed, when she changed, and why she needed to.

She was never prepared to feel the trappings of a daily routine in that sense.

The routine has been upended and she is trying to replace the mess with familiarity.

She knows in her heart it will never be even close to the routine.

She always believed she could adapt to changes in her life, but so unprepared for this one.

She has had to pull back on the curtain of who she is to see who she will become.

She is trying to answer the questions of adaptation, yet still fighting her own ego.

Acceptance does not come easily for her, as the answers are not clear in her head.

"Why?" is continuously in her peripheral vision, and no matter how many times she shakes her head, it is still there.

Letting go of the questions to her being and listening for the answers isn't currently her forte.

That for her is a huge part of her angst and her inability to adapt to the rapid external changes.

She looks in the mirror and she sees her being in who she was at different milestones of her life.

The milestone she isn't looking at is the adaptation that is required right here and right now.

Some part of her obsessive quality right now is being pulled from the fear of "the right thing."

She has been faced with the split of the other half of her and she really has no clue how to be when finding the masculine side of her heart.

"Why now?" is the question *du jour*, and she is searching for the answer knowing full well she already has it.

Her soul has given her answers to her heart but she wants to adapt them to her being or her control.

Her being will keep tripping her if she doesn't slow down and just be one with herself.

She has managed to scrape her knees and elbows being tripped, by acting obtuse.

She has to allow herself to adapt to the person she is becoming and accept that "this too shall pass."

She has always been grounded in who she was and now she needs to shift her soul and being to enjoying herself in all her glory now.

"Why now?" has been answered in the discovery of the masculine side of her heart and the easiness of it.

That is the lack of adaptation as she struggled to live her life by an idea.

She judged the other side of her heart harshly until she has learned she has lived her own life in her own picture of perfection.

She counseled others to let go of the idea yet is being made aware she has lived her own life to date in her own idea.

No matter the circumstances or what happened in her life and beliefs, she adapted the ugly truths to the picture.

The turmoil has quieted as she has learned another tore the picture to shreds and ensured she made the full adaptation to living in her being and enjoying the changing picture.

Grief in a Life

May 24, 2012

It has been raining continuously for what seems like forever.

It has in reality been two and half days, with no let up in sight.

Another has passed from this life to another place in our hearts.

The pain it seems has no ending, nor do we feel any rest.

Our lives as we knew them and lived them for years are but memories gazed upon in hope.

As we touch the people in our lives in love and healing, we know our day is this life.

When the services of the life that has passed are done, we fear the step toward the change.

Words can be said, and the touch is warm and welcomed.

The cold current of air rushes between the touch and reality seeps in.

The goodbyes are shared and the ones left behind leave the sadness of one to their own devices.

The sympathy floats around all that are touched, yet it is felt that one day it will be our sadness of one.

The escape as the door closes behind us is secretly a sigh of relief.

It is another. It is not I.

The passing is shared as the life was shared in fleeting moments.

We have our moments in this life and it is the present of this short time.

When touching another's life we give them hope and warmth of better moments ahead.

Grief overwhelms the head, heart, and soul yet it makes us feel, even if for just a moment.

Grief is not fleeting and can last far longer than it should when letting go.

Our life is the gift, our loved ones the enhancers, friends the extensions, faith the stability, and it is all we need to believe in this life.

We need to grieve to believe in another day and another moment.

Our belief to grief is for what is no longer.

When we see and feel the emotions of loss of what we had, the selfishness of wanting life shows in our strength to endure.

The loss, whether quick or slow, truly pushes our desire for life to the forefront.

As we live in our own judgment we do know we need to keep moving towards our daily goal of living this life.

We all will have our day and those left behind will cry, hurt, and grieve, and will take the next step into their present.

NB – written after the memorial service for Lynne DuHault.

Part of this is in answer to my own grief/grieving for my spouse, David R. Beveridge, who at the time of this writing is terminally ill with vascular dementia.

Crotchety

May 27, 2012

In our youth we think that those angry old people are just mean.

We are indulged by our parents for what they think they missed.

The giving is justified in our brains, as it is easy to just do.

When we stop and take stock of what we give the next generation, we wonder:

Is what they get, going to make them understand their life?

Does easy mean less appreciation and more want of things?

Is working hard the crime of life, or is it the gift of being?

Our time to give and receive changes with our age.

Those mean old folks that we felt were crotchety are arriving at the crossroads of what I gave.

There is more time, in a sense, to see, think, and desire what is left of their lives.

Did we give all away as we were quickly growing into ourselves?

Is the crotchetiness of our older selves just the acceptance we gave too much of our being?

Did we save enough of our lives to be happy within or move on to the next ride in our lives?

In giving away the tiny bits of our thoughts and things, was the cup being replenished?

Have we drunk enough of our life and still allowed love to drink its fill?

How much of us did we allow in the growth of our person?

Have we strangled our mates of choice or accepted to stop feeling emotions that make us whole?

I see my family and I know they think "She is a crotchety old bag."

I know they do as I did to my own direct family.

History repeats itself no matter what, as human nature dictates the process.

We can change "what is" if we can observe it objectively.

When we arrive at the crotchety old stage we understand it is the losses we suffered and what we gave along the way.

We question the life we have led. Whether enjoyed or embittered, our question remains:

Would we have done anything different in anyone's life we encountered?

I know I would not under the same circumstances and even the same results.

I tried daily to live my life to its fullest conclusion and I have succeeded along the way.

I am now a crotchety old person and I earned that badge of honour, as I am here in all my beliefs and desires and know I chose life, always.

I gave, I received, I am thankful, I think, I am, I cry, I have loved, I love still, I give, I want, I desire, and most of all I smile the crotchety old smile.

All will arrive here and when they do, they should smile.

Duty of Disease

June 5, 2012

Today I must do my duty to my spouse.

It does not matter how much I grouse.

One day a few years ago his life with me went away.

At the time I did not see how much of my life turned to grey.

Slowly and surely the distances between us grew.

I did not know what would get me through.

When those distances became blatantly clear,

Our life together became a memory I held dear.

This disease stole more than body, heart, and soul.

It stripped us down to our cores leaving us nakedly bared.

In the progression of deterioration emptiness was the goal.

His heart always knew the strength required would fight all who dared.

His spouse of choice would follow through on his desire,

As he knew she would find the road without being mired.

The steps have been painful when she slipped and fell.

Many times all she wanted was for him to hear her yell.

She could not hide the pain that crossed her face,

As all she wanted was his embrace.

Long before she came into your life as you chose to take a drink,

She feels the results and possibly the link.

Our excesses in our daily living and the disease that has
    stolen so much,

So much put at risk when taken at lunch.

No harm should come from innocent imbibes,

As a simple action should not cause some to die.

The questions begin to flow in her head.

Why does she lose when finally she can see clearly without
    any dread?

My spouse, you have gone from us and left me to ensure
    your comfort.

Daily I do what is necessary, which allows my head and
    heart to sort.

Our lives together were not always perfect.

We worked together for the most part to build and erect.

The foundation is still strong in your spouse but the alone-
    ness overwhelms her stability.

It shakes her core being and then fear chases her desire to
    run.

This was our time together and the moments of laughter,
    tears, and our lives were lived in the light of the sun.

It wasn't perfection at all times but every day was interest-
    ing.

I knew you before the disease took all from you and I am
    betting,

Wherever you are in your soul you are at peace, as you
    lived your life at your pace.

The disease has won this race, but left many memories to
    trace.

The universe has been busy bringing people together when
    needed.

You no longer need me and in that knowledge, I can only
    ensure your care with grace.

My Being
June 8, 2012

My being feels lost and alone in one more change in this trip.

My being never asked for this trip of a lifetime, nor the rides for free.

My being feels nauseated from the whiplash of emotion.

My being was pushed onto the ride and slammed in place.

My being was too dumbfounded to react in any way to the intensity of her feelings.

The ride began as a slow motion in a slightly curved pattern minus any pain.

My being in that 180 degree turn that was so quick felt only a little discomfort.

In the speed of the move my being was turned inside out.

My being looked around and only found one being.

The corners in my being began to curl in a perpetual state of uneasiness.

My being walked and laboured through the abrupt motions of the ride.

My being picked at my routine so there was always a cane of stability.

When my being found itself in despair the ride slowed enough to hear the heart.

My being began its momentum in changing my environment, in which it dwelled.

My being has been tearing at the fabric that only clothed the body.

My being has felt the sheer bareness of looking at what was in the life.

My being knows and has felt every change of requirement to keep the ride from bruising her further.

My being is changing the who of me and has found the itch that needs to be scratched.

My being has let the itch alone for far too many years in obtusity,

My being loved in the manner in which her ideas would be fruitful.

My being worked hard, played a little, had a willing partner, and the elements came together.

My being felt and saw the desired results and enjoyed them.

My being didn't see what was happening to the element that was contributing as well.

My being knew somewhere in her that element was leaving her to her idea.

The ride once again picked up its speed on its way to its descent.

My being knew always that she would respect the wishes of the element and follow through.

My being has walked the miles to nowhere to begin once again.

My being has cried rivers of tears to cleanse once more.

My being has been agitated to levels of pure edge.

My being has been angry enough to need latent anger re-pression therapy.

My being has led to a therapy that has literally soothed the cage so it would hold her gently.

My being understands the gifts that came along in the same space as the nausea of motion.

My being knows this ride will end one day, with the hurt scarred over, the anger healed, and the desire still in place.

This life her being has lived and continues living has at the root of her the positive being to keep being.

Landscapes II
June 14, 2012

The view upon the land has changed once again.

Some of the windrows are gone and buried or burned to cinders.

It doesn't matter which, as both ways they have been returned to the earth.

The land has been opened up and laid bare to receive a different kind of seed.

The new seed will feed and nourish the masses of life.

The cycle is full as the hardiest of weed seed and grass take hold first.

The soil will be tilled a few more times to destroy the rooting of those seeds.

As the rooting disappears and the earth permeates the nutrients, it rests.

While the nutrients seem to be hiding in the till, they silently await the required seed for growth.

The bleakness of the earth when it rests calls to the heart of life.

It desires the seeds of coverage to dress the land in a different beauty.

There is harshness when the land is being torn apart to make room for years of new growth.

There will be new production for food and beverages and things money can buy.

The landscape has been in existence since time began and will continue.

The changes may be drastic at times, as the new growth of the next generations take from the land.

As the new growth appears, will the respect for what is put forth from the seeds be fruitful?

Many beasts will cross this land, and all will leave their mark.

The mark may leave a scar upon the earth while feeding the lives of many.

The scar may show itself for some time while nature heals the brutality of feeding.

The beauty in this landscape is the acceptance of forever changing.

Running

June 28, 2012

The mugginess hangs in the air this morning as I step out for the feel good hormone shot.

When I look to the east the shroud seems like a filmy gauze covering the earth.

The sun tries to peak out and break through as my mind begins the breathing that will be needed to carry me.

The question "Why am I doing this?" assaults my being and I push past the negativity.

It has been years since I did any amount of running and it is taking some time to get back in the groove.

I do this to feel better about life and myself, and the importance of health.

My healthy mind and body are mine to do as I please, and I am choosing exercise for mind and body.

The tightness of muscle in my legs and buttocks is a bit painful but they are still limber.

The soles of my feet ache as I go, but not as a damaging ache.

The ache in my feet tells me I am alive and will survive this run.

Gasping for breath when a short distance is completed tells me more practice is required.

The sweat rolls into the corner of my eyes and the salt stings and my tears wash it away.

As the sun finally breaks the shrouded haze the pain pheromone kicks in and all I feel is good.

My breathing evens out and the sheer pleasure of the exercise feels wonderful.

My thoughts as I find my rhythm are about my breathing, my foot falls, and the goal in my sight.

The running does help me focus on the here and now and what I can do.

I am not sure why I stopped running years ago, but the feeling never quite left me on the good of the action.

The past few months have begun to bring a lot of things back into focus and the running and exercise help.

It is today that I have completed a run and I am thankful I could execute this run this day.

Impacts

July 7, 2012

An illusion of a single event in a person's life creates the impact.

It will shatter the glass cage we build for ourselves and that we exist in.

Seeing the point of impact is such a tiny mark. You don't really focus on the spot.

One day there is a hairline crack extending from the spot and you notice.

The next time you see the crack it is longer and going in a different direction.

When you have been busy living, you have forgotten to see the change in the mark.

As we put one foot in front of the other to keep the forward momentum, we forget the value of our actions.

As the web of cracks move in a pattern of unawareness, our lives are being impacted with every new break.

We should stop and look around us and comprehend what we do.

We do what our family, friends, and society dictate for the greater good.

Every one of those cracks is a member of what society dictates and when the impact began

Gathering the pieces of the puzzle in those cracks and receiving some intelligent information only happens when you feel the impact.

Starting at the point of you and flowing outwards, you be-
gin to realize the universal truth.

Nature and our instinct are what guide each of us.

Blinded by our own angst and others in our universe, we
miss the point of sharing.

When given the actuality of a person telling you what the
impact has been, then you catch a glimpse.

When deciphering the pattern of the shattering glass, only
then do you understand a portion of who you are.

As life begins the process of replacing and repairing the
cracks you feel wholeness return to you.

It is the decision you make with head or heart that defines a
whole new you.

Stepping back away from the point of impact you can see
every connection ever made.

Refusing to look and feel the whole impact leaves you for-
ever looking through the cracks in our lives.

Only we can view the impact and it is up to others how they
feel when looking through their own shattered cages.

The influence of one and the impact on others is astounding
when viewed as a whole.

Landscapes More
July 17, 2012

When driving onto the section that has been brushed to renewal,

The overwhelming smell permeating the air and Mother Earth is the smell of dead fire and smoke.

It smells of the changes that have happened to this land in the past year.

The smell almost has a sickly sweet taste in the back of your throat.

Smoldering embers may be the heaviness in the air of the smell surrounding me as I write.

The roots in clumps that lay atop the soil have the sense of small bumps in our lives that we mow over and feel but never notice.

Bits of rock and pieces of wood that didn't get burned or chewed up are dots between the clumps.

Some are charred and chipped and all sizes that will take longer to break down and become nutrition for the soil.

The blackened earth from the fires will lessen and blend to earth once more.

Ash sets lightly on the soil where the rain has packed it firmly.

The trees that no longer are sparse and jumbled on the section tell the story of change.

Gently rolling inclines throughout this section tell me even Mother Earth hiccupped in the birth of her land.

The inclines are like our lives gently rolling or an immediate drop.

It is the negotiation of the drops and inclines and the even keels that define our ability to live life to the utmost.

Once in a while the curve in the landscape is so subtle we see, feel, and know, yet we struggle.

Our fear of the unknown is so strong we allow ourselves to be stuck in the mire we created for ourselves.

When the smoke triggers the fire, you move away from the ash, the heat, and the toxicity in the smoke.

It is not the move to safety away from the smoke—it is the choice of direction we take.

The landscape has changed once again out of necessity by another's desire for collection.

Mother Earth's son has had his way with the female entity in his being to change what he sees and what he needs.

The sanctity of Mother Earth is a lesson not learned by many.

He still wants to plow, disc, cultivate, burn, brush, and bulldoze the emotions away.

Mother Earth can only embrace and give the nutrients needed to feed and soothe.

It is up to us to breathe in the smoke and clear it in ourselves when we finally breathe out.

The wind has picked up and the smoke is less heavy as I clear my own landscape.

One day he will comprehend the breath of love given in the simplest of gestures.

Touch the landscape and you forever change the view of what you see and all others after.

Dominance

July 19, 2012

The state of hormones subtly flows through the room as he enters.

There is no tension or mood previous to that entrance.

An innocent question asked by another instilled a need to push the other away.

The power of a thought and the reaction by others and they had no true sense of what hit them, metaphorically.

The hackles were up upon seeing others viewing his assumed domain.

The domain he feels has her own senses that need to be satisfied and they will do exactly that.

She has been told often enough that no matter what, all others are more important.

The domain has decided to fight back to satisfy her base needs as a woman.

There is nothing perfect in her world and she is taking care to look better and feel luscious.

The domain can push the dominant just enough to get his testosterone up and working.

There is no need to touch, as they both are terribly aware of each other.

Dominance has been shot out there continuously for a while now and the domain senses his presence.

Furtive looks are seen by all others that are in the room and the looks on those faces question.

As the estrogen and testosterone build in each of them, the static is becoming sharper.

The domain is finding it more difficult to control the desire where it burns hot.

The dominant has got such an iron grip on his desire that it slips out when least expected.

The dominant has managed to chase away the most innocent bystanders.

Instinct takes over even when all seems correct.

The odours that seep into the air being exuded from the domain when the dominant is present are palatable.

They only lie to themselves by forcing the picture that all must see.

This has been such a display of hormones that I am taken aback by the intensity.

Contact with others in their space feels that all is not as it looks.

The static pushed is smelled and tasted in each other's beings.

The Parade

August 11, 2012

Small town anywhere gathers neighbours and friends to honour the past and present.

The gazebo is full of people enjoying the pancakes cooked by the volunteers.

It stormed before the parade so the grass is damp but the spirits are happy.

The sun is out and blazing down on the route for people to see.

A small donation to keep the past in good repair.

The summer of parades and fairs to celebrate the community annually.

A moment in time when all seems right with the universe for the span of a few hours.

They speak quietly as there really are no others to break the tone they hear.

Once a year the community pulls together to honour and respect what came before.

It is a gaudy float, horseback riders, pipes, and jesters, and not all in the parade.

This is my first small town anywhere parade in years and when I was young I saw only what was in my path.

My work is done that is critical, and I can take my time to write this prose.

My spirit is lighter in doing this, as taking this time is important to my soul.

Will anyone understand what I see and hear and try to describe?

Sitting quiet I hear the murmurs of talking, the barking of dogs, the purring of engines, and the patter of young feet in a hurry to go anywhere.

Being alone in a crowd is more enlightening than being part of the crowd.

You are more than a part of the whole. You are a whole in part of the entirety.

The simplest float requires the imagination of the community in which it thrives.

The horses and carriages of the past make us think of simpler times.

The times were no simpler then than now; just different hurdles to move.

The wagons used for travel and hauling of commodities are different, but the cost is the same.

The horse riders amble along the same as always. Now they may have more glitter.

As the parade passes before me I am restless in the simplicity of what I have seen of small town anywhere.

This parade has been a lesson in being focused on the immediate changes that have happened and enjoying the tiniest moments in life.

Imagine Senses

August 9, 2012

We feel, but we do not touch.

We see, but we do not look.

We hear, but we do not listen.

We think, but we do not act.

We smell, but we do not sniff.

We do so many things by rote that we forget to think about what we do.

The last step you took—did you feel the vibration throughout your core?

Upon awakening in the night, did you see the darkness around you?

When your feet hit the floor, did you take the moment and feel the smoothness?

Did you sense every step to where you are going in the darkness?

Was the quiet overwhelming to your being?

Did your hand touch the bed to know when to turn and crawl back into the softness?

When you breathed, did you smell the scent of the oils and odours of yourself?

In the firmness of laying down in the comfort, did you just be?

Was sleep simple in returning or did thoughts run amok until you reigned them in?

There in the darkness before the dawn as I have seen this
many times in the past year,

I wondered, "Has my reality changed so much that I am
more sensitive in my awareness?"

I know I live daily even when it seems as if I do not.

The music in my soul is louder than it has ever been.

The vibrations of others are felt and acknowledged even
without realizing it.

These vibrations have sunk me into the black abyss of emo-
tions.

They have made me so nauseated I thought I would be sick.

Those people that are so strong in their vibrations know I
am receiving the message.

I have had to block the one vibration, as it was dragging the
life from me.

The other one that is so strong will stop when the acknowl-
edgment of his needs, wants, and love is accepted by
him.

The amazing ability to feel, see, want, acknowledge, and be
every day is so much more than the present.

Living isn't easy all of the time but it is all we have, and if
we can think kindly now, life is a joy.

I Feel

August 11, 2012

As I move from the drastic changes to the seemingly smoother ones, I feel.

As I have changed with life's changes, I feel.

As I moved from home to heart, I feel.

As I learned to cry with sadness, I feel.

As I learned to laugh with pleasure, I feel.

As I took one step further than before, I feel.

As I look ahead and to the side, I feel.

As the incline becomes steeper in the climb, I feel.

At the peak of the incline I stop to breathe. I feel.

As the momentum carries me forward faster than anticipated, I feel.

As I rest in the next movement, I feel.

As I watch the changes in my body and mind, I feel.

As the muscle builds in my legs and torso, I feel.

As I sit and write and wonder what life has next for me, I feel.

As I listen to wind blow through the trees and grass, I feel.

As I smell the air and feel it expand my lungs, I feel.

As I listen to the thunder of Mother Nature, I feel.

As the lightning flashes and lights the early morning sky, I feel.

As I pet my dogs to calm their anxiety of the storm, I feel.

As I roll once more in my sleeplessness, I feel.

As I watch fluffy clouds roll across the sky, I feel.

As my emotions take me on a roller coaster ride, I feel.

As I sit here in the middle of open land and fields, I feel.

As I go about my daily life, I feel.

As the sun beats down on my shoulders, I feel.

As it warms the skin it also warms my soul and feeds me the desire to feel.

As I have arrived at this stage in my life, I feel.

As I look at my hands and see the length of my fingers, I feel.

As I move my feet in the grass, I feel.

As I move to the next stage of growth and change, I want to continue to feel.

I have come to realize that in my life, along the way, I have always allowed myself to feel.

Conquering

August 12, 2012

Sitting on the beast that scraped and ripped the land apart to renew,

In that secret hiding place in all mankind the ego of conquering sneaks in.

The woman in me has a healthy respect for the gifts of Mother Earth, including the one I am beginning to live, and that is strength.

This beast and the man who operates it have conquered my heart and the land in me.

It has been pushing the land and my desire to be conquered to its absolute naked soul.

I cannot be anymore stripped than this land. The rock beneath has been exposed to the elements of servitude.

The being in me has the urge to rip and tear this beast down to the core.

This land is living and dying every moment as I find myself doing.

Some of me is charred and ash.

Some of the land in me is fallow and some is lush and flourishing.

There are gallons of moisture as my river of renewal flows.

The rocks and sticks I find myself tripping on is nature saying, "Go a little slower and be."

As the land of my heart heals and fights back to grow abundantly, so does love.

As the end of this quarter of land gets picked of rock, disced to turn the roots, and swept by distraction, will the beast have cleared his head?

The black soil has been laid bare but the soul of the land still lives.

My emotions about my heart cannot be destroyed by either beast, as Mother Nature always takes care of her own.

Life as it was is behind us, as it is under us, and as it changes in front as far as the desire for life can be.

Secrets

August 12, 2012

Who is damaged the most when the secret escapes the confines?

Is it shame the reason a secret is kept?

Is it embarrassment for self or friends and family?

Is it so dark and appalling that you have made it that way in your mind?

Is it a mole hill that has been made into a mountain by your judgment or that of others?

Is it truth only to you and did harm come to another?

Is it something that another holds with a tight grip over your well-being?

Is it information that will cost you your standing within you?

Is the secret carried forward in your children or are they allowed to leave it behind?

Is the secret you will pay with monetary or emotional?

Is the secret done as a child and no one really knows any better?

Is the secret done as an adult and more than you got hurt?

A secret is only something you may have done. Did you, and you knew better?

When there are no secrets there is no shame or embarrassment or harassment from others.

Society will always judge others by their own individual secrets.

Judgment is not for us to squander or to beat others for their humanity.

A secret to one would not be to another, and the only ones that truly know, know that society is keeping the secrets.

We have the laws and societal rules that allow us to live freely and know what we should and shouldn't do.

Morality is society's judgment of behaviour, perceived or actual.

Society really only wants to do what the person with the so-called secrets is doing.

Living when the secrets are gone, so goes society's need to judge and rule about others behaviours.

Showers

September 5, 2012

As the water cascades down the falls of my body, I change.

The past gets swept away with the flow of water cleaning the present.

The feeling of the moisture renewing the cells of myself clears my thoughts.

The heat in the water soothes my skin and feels warm to my inner self.

My daily shower takes on movement that is ingrained partially out of habit.

The many times in my life that showering was just part of my day,

I did not notice how it really made me feel.

The shampoo on my hands feels silky and running my fingers through the strands, I notice the texture.

The hair feels rough but squeaky clean.

The conditioner feels slightly slimy yet once massaged into the hair the satin smoothness returns.

Soaping my body and with the lack of fragrance in the soap, I only sense myself.

There is a slight roughness to the stubble on my legs that feels natural to who I am.

The shower makes me squeaky smooth with just enough roughness to make me interesting.

Readiness

September 11, 2012

I wasn't ready for my heart to implode looking at you.

I wasn't ready to trip over my breath when you stole it away.

I wasn't ready to look into the mirror and have you seem so loving.

I wasn't ready to have the intensity run rampant in me.

I wasn't ready to be with you with so much else going on.

I wasn't ready to watch the possession of my heart.

I wasn't hurt by the brutal honesty in your fear.

I wasn't ready to deal with your unexpected guilt about loving me.

I wasn't ready not to feel your arms holding me close.

I wasn't ready to hear you say "I'm scared silly."

I wasn't ready when you held me gently.

I wasn't ready at the whisper of a simple kiss.

I wasn't ready for the change in me.

I wasn't ready to desire to be nowhere else on earth but in your arms.

I wasn't ready to feel the peace in me knowing I met the love of my life.

I wasn't ready to acknowledge that one thing I thought I was prepared for. I was not.

I wasn't ready to move into the love that had been waiting for years.

I am finally ready. Now you are not.

Neither of us was prepared to sever the readiness.

While I struggled, you waited to share your heart.

It is my turn at readiness while you struggle with your heart.

Our cry, our hearts, and our love will continue until readiness is at hand and beyond.

A Moment in Harvest

September 17, 2012

The rows are all neat and tidy and all evenly spaced.

It is a puzzle that if pushed together would give you the true lay of the land.

There are gentle twists and turns as the bounty cures in its pods to be pounded out of the coat.

The colour changes from the green of plant to the shiny colour of money.

When tarnished the correct colour of tan the harvest begins.

The brown seeds of plants sometimes escape to grow in place upon renewal of the seasons.

The rumble of equipment on the land and the operators go unnoticed.

It is just the continuous vibrations of living on the land.

The stalks are sharp and will make you bleed if you're not careful walking about them.

It will take Mother Earth to break them down for fodder to replenish her womb to grow the next child of the season.

She will feed, clothe, and entertain the masses as she has over the test of time.

She is so hardy that we stop understanding that she may crumble but she will not fail.

The learned of this earth know that you can change some things but the basics never change.

Appreciation of the harvest is momentary, as life moves about us as it does the land.

The rewards we end with are monetary, and the truth of
   working with Mother Nature shows as such.

We may feel an affinity with the soul of the land, but are we
   intelligent enough to know ourselves.

The labour of love of the farm and the effort put forth
   comes to fruition as the frost begins and the snow flies.

A new season of rest begins and the sigh of Mother Earth
   can be heard in the howl of the wind.

A thank you for Mother Earth in the wisdom of true belief
   as the harvest ends.

Movement in Dirt

September 23, 2012

The trudge of movement senses the need of going forth.

The dirt curls around the foot with even measured pushing outward.

It makes room for the feet to be planted firmly in the soil and hold firm.

Uneven paths cross one another to lead the way.

I follow and know not where they lead, only the certainty of trust in my being.

We will celebrate the life we have and embrace the breath we are given.

Sometimes labour is about the hardness of beginning to change.

Letting go of the energy is in the desire to experience more.

The bounty can and usually is most enjoyed when we stop and let life flow with us.

The silt of soil forces itself in the shoes and scrapes the skin in steps taken.

The wind soothes the body from the exertion of discovery.

The air has a strong odour of dust and harvest.

Our sun is a slight bit less in its heat intensity and the plants change as they cool.

As the season of fall begins, so does the urge to slow my emotional upheaval.

My patience within me has pushed me beyond what I need in the seasons of my love.

My lessons in life are being rewarded with remembrance of the life I lived and gave.

The fertility of my imagination is in the forefront and I feel the push from the universe to express my heart.

My procreated being is my chance to leave a part of me in him.

My intelligence and wordiness is my obligation to my ability of heartfelt expression.

Not all will care or even read me, yet I hope those who will use this as pause for thought.

Words are my season and I will traverse them all with the spirit of difference.

It may engage a discussion or a thought of "Who was this being?"

I am a creature of this universe who has finally let her heart be.

For a Wiser Friend

October 5, 2012

A tea has turned into thoughts of how fast our lives can change.

The single person that can trigger questions never asked but wondered:

Did the person want to express those answers but no one asked?

Has the chance to ask and be answered gone forever in a fall?

Should our lives be so narrow in focus that we stop wondering?

Would we change our direction if we knew the answers from where we came?

Will the opportunity present itself to ask the wise the important information?

Who were you in the life you led and gave to others?

Were you the person everyone saw and knew?

Were you the person, the parent, the friend, the lover, the family you contributed to, in guiding their person?

Did societal views hamper the willingness to love another?

The shortness of our time here has been roosting in my heart and pushing me to discover my own desires to push past what has held me back.

The power of faith in life leads the wonderment and joy to believe anything is possible.

As healing begins, the faith keeps you stable. You will recover and your children will reap the rewards of having you near.

We forget more than we remember, and our lives are granted a short time.

In knowing you so little, you touched the core of me with "I'm not needed anymore!"

Someone will always need you, and remember, your living has touched so deeply.

This is the second time in my life I have been given the opportunity to tell fathers, "I am glad it was you," and see the understanding in those few words.

Tea will still be brewing when next the opportunity arises.

The Abyss

November 2, 2012

A day arrives when no matter what has happened before,

You know what goes forward is what you need to focus on.

I have lived my life according to my heart and faith.

It has been a good life and any pain that has mattered has been handled.

There has been fun, humour, love, friends, husbands, children, family,

A hand held when needed, a smile through any tears.

Extend yourself when someone else is in more despair than your own perception.

Lending an ear can heal a tiny spot in another's life, unexpectedly.

The roller coaster of the emotional abyss has whipped me into submission, as I avoided it throughout my life.

The drops into the abyss are trying to teach me it is alright to feel.

Stepping up to the plate and facing my fears, I am learning we all fear the abyss.

Allowing others to see the vulnerability that surrounds me, I have learned it enhances their own abyss.

My lip may sound harsh and unrepentant about life most times.

It is me learning to live forward with no "Would have, should have, could have."

I made any decision to the best of my circumstance and what I understood at the time.

"My life! My risk! I did!"

No permission asked or answered, yet I shared the importance of my being.

The starkness of my reality still is "I did and I still do," and will forever.

Live Widow

November 26, 2012

My journey to being a live widow has been the scariest part of my life.

I realized in becoming a live widow I do not know how to move forward.

I cannot give freely to another knowing I am tied to my ward till I become the widow.

My faith and beliefs are so strong that I do not understand how to sever them to change.

Moving forward for this live widow means looking into the mirror for support and honesty.

Being a live widow is a painful journey into aloneness and loneliness.

No one else can get the live widows through this, as they won't let someone else in, knowing there is no hope or future.

Live widows know in their core there is so much more pain to get through.

Activity keeps them moving but not loving anyone special.

Live widows exist while their own personal pain gets deciphered until understanding becomes the norm.

Live widows have to learn that they will never receive the comprehension from the person that made them a live widow.

The live widows must find their own personal strength to keep their morale from drowning in the change.

Acceptance of live widowhood is fought daily and momentarily it feels like insanity.

The crack in the live widow seems like it is getting larger instead of healing.

Daily, the live widow must make sense out of incomprehension and hold it together as well.

The live widow lives in the grey area between breathing and living.

Moving continuously is the only outlet the live widow has just to cope.

The live widows know they must never give up and stop, for the fear will slowly kill the spirit to live.

Life's Lottery

December 6, 2012

The moment we open our eyes in the morning, we cut the ace of spades.

The movement of throwing back the covers and our feet hitting the floor, we cut the ace of clubs.

The first step towards our day and we know the cut of the ace of diamonds.

Sitting across from your love or your children, we really know the cut of the ace of hearts.

Savouring the taste of a cup of tea or coffee you feel like the king of your castle.

Momentarily the thought passes through the brain that the queen will rule the king for position and caring.

As the jacks take their spot in the funding trades of incomes we know security.

It is the tens of jobs we need to do daily that can overwhelm.

The nine hours of day we toil for our employment.

Eight moments of quiet we take when given a smile unexpectedly.

The luck of the lottery of life may span the thought of "What if a lucky seven rolled our way?"

Six people daily touch our lives without our knowledge of the reason they moved about our being.

In the next five minutes our lives have once again played the lottery in life.

The complete evenness of four takes a journey of insight upon breathing.

Me, myself, and I make three times the ego of what our life lottery shakes out.

Two give the odds that with another we will be more than simplicity.

One is where the lottery of our lives begins and grows so much and so little in the many nuances of living.

The luck of the draw is that we exist in this reality.

A Thought for You

December 27, 2012

Thoughts in time are your heart and the gift of life.

Every day you listen to your head and do the work that needs to be done.

A few times a day you find yourself doing for others.

The list of "to do" that you have in your head overwhelms the time frame of one day.

The twenty-four hours you live seem split into too little.

When you change the time in your doing what needs to be done, you feel a little lost to shortage of time in your day.

The thought of "I want to be alone" when others are pulling at your strengths creeps in unexpectedly.

No one understands you as you trusted once and it has been bashed so thoroughly the powder clogs the path which is open to you.

The religion you believed so deeply in contributed to helping you to cement your heart against ever trusting again.

The road to hell is paved with good intentions and not following your heart is also a path less chosen.

Intent is the thought and intend is the process. Doing neither is the loss.

Faith is the one true constant in our reality, as without it there would be no life as we know it.

Faith is the all-encompassing belief in all positive energy of our being.

All is possible when you have faith in heart and yourself.

All is probable when we are willing to change and complete the work required.

Who in your time and space is hindering and who is helping, or is there only acceptance of less than heart?

Yourself, your heart, your responsibility, your care, your family, your control—

Take you back, along with all the risk and reward that goes along with it.

I see, I want, I buy!

The dress you wear daily was purchased with the lie and you wear it daily, knowing it didn't fit then, that it doesn't now, and that you never liked it.

Like so many closets, yours is full of window dressing that should never have been purchased and fully refunded upon return.

Finally, you walked by the window showcasing the perfect dress and the price of the perfect fit is out of your reach.

The price tag says "Not for Sale." This item can only be purchased with love and worn with warmth.

When looking closely at the seams you will find these words sewn: "Not for Everyone!"

Morning to a New Year

December 31, 2012

The warmth of the line across the sky is in clear definition.

It is a white and yellow line between space and clouds.

The ripples in the clouds are of sky blue to ocean blue to pinkish-yellow.

The Neapolitan of the sight pushes our hearts to the desirableness of ourselves.

The crust is firm but flaking while supporting the emotions of heart.

Beautiful cream melts into the senses of taste, smell, and the core of growth.

The top is the icing of our lives and the artsy wonderful patterns of delight.

Every bite changes the pattern we feel and the moments of the sky change as the sun bites through our time.

There is a shadow on the crust as a moment changes everything.

The sky has evolved to a grayish-mauve blanket that hides the sheen temporarily.

The white and yellow lace on the blanketed sky hides the truths that have accumulated without us seeing.

The heart of the sun peaks under the layers and in between our senses.

As the sun pushes back the blanket of us and warms our wants and needs,

Clarity on the slight breeze rolls over the humanness of our
   life.

It whispers that we are our lives and so should we always
   be.

As the morning changes the Neapolitan layers to yet an-
   other variety of flavour to experience with sparkles of
   ice, we are.

CPSIA information can be obtained at www.ICGtesting.com
Printed in the USA
LVOW08s0744091214

417840LV00001B/33/P